Do Bad Guys Wear Socks?

Living the Gospel in Everyday Life

by M. Regina Cram

for my parents,
who filled my childhood
with love and laughter

Acknowledgments

Chapters of this book first appeared in *The Catholic Transcript*, the newspaper of the Archdiocese of Hartford. Therefore I owe unending gratitude to Fr. Chris Tiano, Roberta Tuttle, Elisa Krochmalnykyj, Leslie DiVenere, Jack Sheedy, and Msgr. David Q. Liptak, and a decade of proofreaders. Many thanks.

I also owe thanks to my first fans, Mirja Johanson, Pat Peck and Susan Bailey. Your encouragement kept me going for years. Thanks to Evan Cogswell for walking me through the technical mysteries. Thanks, too, to Frs. John Gwozdz, Tom Hickey, Jeffrey Romans, John Melnick, Kevin Cavanaugh, Arthur DuPont, and Kevin Forsyth. And of course, Marilyn "Dickie" Hopper and Carla Ruiz.

I could never have succeeded without our parents, Patricia and Hank Petrilli, the late Herbert Waite, Mary Louise and the late Harkness Cram, and our siblings, Ginny and Mike Martin, the late Marietta Tierney Waite, Katherine "Tenna" Cram, and Rick Cram.

Most especially, a loving thanks to Peter "Skip" and Kaitlyn Cram, Meredith and Chris Dresko, Tierney and Andrew Keogler, and Victoria Cram and Shane Smith. My deepest thanks go to Peter Harkness Cram, whom I love with all my heart.

Unconditional Love

for Michael Gradone

It was a hot summer day at the Post Office as I juggled parcel, baby, purse, and the grip of two preschoolers. We were mailing a care package to a state prison where my sister Marietta was an inmate.

That's when 3-year old Meredith piped up. "Mama?" she said in that sweet voice of innocence. "Is Auntie Etta a bad guy?"

Good question. What was a good answer?

I was 2 years, 4½ months older than my sister, and as a kid I never let her forget it. I was a know-it-all and she was a pest, and we argued until I thought my parents would go crazy. I used to brag that I was much smarter than she was; she'd retaliate by broadcasting that I was the only girl she knew who wore a concave bra. It didn't help that I was a neat freak and she was a free spirit; even the line down the middle of the bedroom didn't stop the bickering. She was always borrowing my clothes and stuffing them under her bed, and I'd find them a week later just when I needed them for something special.

But sometimes we played imaginary games in the dark, and when we were older, we'd play guitar and sing really funny songs until my dad howled and we broke out laughing so hard we couldn't keep singing.

Eventually my sister and I became great friends. She made me laugh, and I helped her believe in herself. She often worked at rehabilitation centers and convalescent homes, and when things got dull she would tell jokes and arrange wheelchair races down the halls. Whenever I visited, I could always find my sister by the sounds of the patients' laughter.

But my sister made a really stupid mistake when she was 12 years old: she took a sip of beer. "It's only one sip," she told herself. "What harm can one little sip do?" But then it was two sips, then a whole can, and the next year she took that first puff of marijuana. By 14 she was doing hard drugs, and running away from home, and flunking out of school.

That's how it was for 20 years, cross-addicted to drugs and alcohol. Twenty years is such a terribly long time. For my sister, it was twenty years of drinking in disgusting bars with people she thought were her friends but who disappeared as soon as the money ran out. It was 20 years of shooting up drugs in burned-out buildings where rats live, getting money any way she could in order to buy that next fix. It was 20 years of missing Thanksgiving dinner because she was too hung over, and sleeping in the back of someone's car when it was five degrees outside, and spending money on drugs instead of buying food for her baby.

For me, it was 20 years of telephone calls at two o'clock in the morning when she screamed at me because I would not give her money for drugs. It was 20 years of wondering if she were alive or dead; and visiting her in the state prison; and having to explain to my children why Auntie Etta never remembered their birthdays.

By the end, my visits were to a residence where people with AIDS go to live, and really, where they go to die. Together we laughed about childhood stories, like the time Georgie Livingston across the street hit my other sister over the head with a baseball bat because he had a crush on her, and how my grandmother used to keep a big plastic skeleton in the attic and always told us that it was Grampy. Sometimes we'd sing favorite songs until other residents yelled at us to stop and we got laughing too hard to keep singing anyway.

And somehow we tried to say good-bye. My sister told me how stupid she had been to start taking drugs and how unbelievably strong was the addiction. I told her how much I wanted to grow old together so we could share a room in the nursing home with an imaginary line down the middle. She said I should have 10 kids and I told her to mind her own business, and together we grieved for a future that would never be.

I wasn't thinking about any of this that hot summer day at the post office.

Hassled by the heat and the baby's squirming, Meredith jerked me out of my reverie with her question about whether Auntie Etta was a bad guy.

Breathing a quick prayer for wisdom, I answered

with the first coherent thing that came to mind. "Well, Meredith, Auntie Etta has done some bad things but God still loves her."

Meredith thought about that for a moment, then said, "You mean God loves it when Auntie Etta does bad things?"

Maybe this was going to be harder than I thought. I reminded Meredith of the recent trouble we'd had with her whining. "Do Mama and Daddy like it when you whine?" I asked. "No," she mumbled with downcast eyes. "Do we love you anyway?" I pressed. "Oh yes!" she quickly exclaimed.

"Well, Sweetheart, it's the same with Auntie Etta," I continued. "It makes God sad when she does bad things, but God still loves her very much and He always will."

"Oh." Silence. "So we should love her too, right, Mama?"

In that quiet moment, Meredith grasped the Gospel story: despite our rebelliousness, God still loves us. And He sent His Son to prove it.

I've Brought You Tonight's Supper

for Bishop Peter Rosazza, who preaches the gospel
by serving the poor

Peter and I had been wrestling with a difficult passage in the Old Testament book of Isaiah. God had told His people that their fasting was unacceptable because it was not accompanied by righteous living, especially in their dealings with the underprivileged. "Is not this the fast that I choose," God had asked, "to share your bread with the hungry, and bring homeless poor into your house; when you see the naked, to clothe him, and not to hide yourself from your own flesh?"

We struggled with this issue of social action. We didn't have much contact with the oppressed people of the world, and to be honest, our lives were pretty comfortable. We went to work, volunteered at church, and helped the poor through our checkbook. It was all quite sanitary. Even if I wanted to help – and I wasn't sure I did – how could I shelter the homeless or feed the hungry if I had constructed my life in such a way as to insulate myself from the very people I was supposed to help?

Still, I could not ignore God's clear directive so I

simply asked Him to show me where to start. I certainly didn't know.

A few weeks later, Peter returned from a business luncheon with packages of unopened cold cuts that he'd been directed to bring home. In the ensuing days we ate turkey sandwiches, ham quiche, chef salad, and every variety of cold cut dishes ever devised, plus a few new ones.

By the end of the week, I never wanted to see another cold cut again, but the supply seemed to be multiplying inside our refrigerator. When Sunday morning rolled around, I glanced at the packages and breathed one of those silent prayers: "Lord, what am I doing to do with all this food?"

That was all I said. Then I headed to church.

Late that afternoon, I began to absent-mindedly chop turkey for yet another chef salad that I had no intention of eating. When I was done, I looked at it and groaned, "Why did I just do that?"

Then a woman came to mind. Her name was Anna and her husband was dying. They were only in their 30s but they looked twice that age after years of illness and hardship. They had a teenage son who sometimes accompanied them to church, but mostly I just saw Anna, always cheerful and quick to encourage those who needed a kind word or a helping hand. Anna's husband had just been hospitalized, and since caring for him had made it impossible for Anna to hold down a job, I suspected that she was struggling to put food on the table. They lived just a mile or two away so, without much thought, I stuffed the chef salad into a brown paper bag, strapped the kids into their car seats, and headed into the late afternoon winter darkness.

When we pulled up to Anna's house, the children clambered to accompany me to the door. Grabbing the bag and the pajama-clad children, I walked up the steps and rang the bell.

Anna opened the door and stared at us blankly. I quickly thrust the bag into her hands and blurted out, "Here. I've brought you tonight's supper."

As soon as the words were spoken, I regretted them. How condescending they sounded, as if I were Superwoman rescuing a damsel in distress.

Anna just stood there. She stared at the children, glanced inside the paper bag, then stared at us again. Tears began to well up in her eyes, and the story spilled out. After church that morning, Anna had gone to the hospital to spend the day at her husband's side. She had not even stopped to eat. Just moments earlier, Anna had arrived home ravenously hungry, but when she'd walked into the kitchen, there was no food. Knowing her circumstances, I think she meant that literally. So she had quietly prayed, "Lord, what am I going to do for tonight's supper?"

At that moment, the doorbell had rung. When Anna opened the door, a woman on the edge of darkness handed her a bag with the words, "Here. I've brought you tonight's supper."

Anna and her son received dinner that night, but I gained the greater treasure. God had brought hungry people into my life, and He had even provided the food for their meal.

All I'd had to provide was the brown paper bag.

When Dying Comes Before Living

for Cynthia Gault and Pam Kolakowski

They were quiet, decent people who were new to the parish. It was Easter night, and their much-wanted second child was anxious to be born. The nursery was ready. The toddler was excited, although she wasn't exactly sure what she was excited about.

But a terrible complication arose, and the baby lived for only 10 days.

During the days while the mother was in the hospital recuperating from emergency surgery, she was anxious to talk with someone – anyone – about her grief. Unfortunately, she and her husband were so new to the area that they had no friends, and their families lived across the country. The husband didn't know what else to do, so he contacted the coordinator of the parish Young Mothers Group and begged her to send women to visit his wife. Anyone. Please.

So the young mothers came, their palms sweaty and their mouths dry, wondering what on earth they could say to a stranger whose baby was dying. The answer, of course, was 'nothing.' But they could listen, which they did. They could send meals and call to encourage and scoop up the toddler for a few hours. And they could pray that the family would begin to heal.

That's what they did.

Some of the women couldn't face the prospect of visiting the hospital so they provided childcare for those who could. It became a team effort.

It was my turn to visit on the second day. I entered the hospital room nervously, introduced myself, then listened quietly as the mother poured out her heart about the beautiful baby boy down the hall, so perfect and yet so near death. Together we wept.

Ten days later, the mothers attended the funeral. It took my breath away when the tiny white coffin, no bigger than an end table, was carried into the near-empty church. Thank God the mothers were there.

Many years have passed and the family still grieves. Nevertheless, they've never forgotten how the Body of Christ wrapped them in kindness during the worst days of their lives. It's funny; at the time we didn't think of ourselves as the Body of Christ. We were just a bunch of terrified moms trying to soften the grief of two broken hearts.

A year or two later another couple in the parish learned that their unborn child had a fatal heart defect and would live for only a day or two after birth. Despite strong pressure from doctors and friends, the couple was adamant about continuing the pregnancy. For two long months, the mothers group was their link with sanity, once again enveloping the family in love. Moms brought meals, sent notes, helped them contact other couples who had suffered similar tragedy, and prayed around the clock.

When the woman went into labor, the phone tree sprung into action. And then, in silence and with desperately heavy hearts, we kept a vigil with them as their little one died.

Fortunately the mothers group shared many celebrations as well. We nearly burst with joy when a tiny redheaded bundle was adopted by a couple whose wait had seemed interminable. A woman who'd been told she would never bear children gave birth to two tiny miracles. A teenage mother was cared for beyond her wildest dreams as women provided clothing, a car seat, babysitting, and moral support.

In jubilation and in tragedy, the mothers have cared for one another, sometimes across many miles. When I miscarried a twin and was confined to bed as we moved out of the area, women from that mothers group arranged for meals to be delivered to us half a state away. Such kindness is not easily forgotten.

But perhaps the mothers' greatest gift has been the love offered to grieving families. People often don't know what to say in such situations, so they stay away and do nothing at all. The young mothers, who lack words just like everyone else, simply offer love. And never is it more needed than when dying comes before living.

Stealing Christmas

for Stephanie Holmes

It was Christmas week 1968 and I was a scrawny seventh-grade kid with too much time, not enough imagination, and a desperate desire to fit in. Ah, the good old days.

One afternoon I went snooping in my mother's closet, hoping to locate her secret stash of Christmas gifts for us kids. Sure enough, there it was behind the stockpile of ugly flowered hats. Before I could investigate further, however, I heard footsteps on the stairs below. I quickly escaped to my room without detection.

A few days later when the house was empty, I crept back into the closet (I hope my mother isn't reading this), grabbed all the boxes marked for me, and smuggled them into my bedroom. There I spent a delightful afternoon of juvenile delinquency as I checked out my gifts. I unwrapped the mood ring and the Flower Power diary and the lava lamp. I tried on the hiphugger bell-bottoms and fishnet stockings, even preening in front of the hall mirror for full effect. Then I carefully re-wrapped my loot and returned it to the closet. (Come to think of it, I hope my kids

15

don't read this, either.)

The next day at school I was a hero. I bragged about my audacity and how I was the only kid in Swampscott, Massachusetts to swipe all my presents. My friends envied my fishnet stockings and I, a shy kid not accustomed to the limelight, reveled in the fleeting popularity. I knew this would be the best Christmas ever.

It was the worst Christmas ever. When the big morning arrived I had to feign surprise while my parents and sisters reveled in the exchange of love. I hadn't chosen love at all; I had chosen myself, and that's exactly what I got. It was a pretty small package.

I never did it again. Over the years I came to understand that Christmas cannot be stolen, nor can it be stashed away behind attic stairs and flowered hats. In fact, Christmas cannot be taken at all; it can only be given away, and it all began when God gave away the most awesome Christmas gift the world has ever known.

It must have seemed an unlikely gift – a squawking baby born to unmarried villagers in a damp animal barn. But things are not always as they appear. How could the world know that this helpless child would pierce the darkness and defeat the forces of evil for all times?

But now we know. Christmas cannot be stolen. It can only be given away, and God in His tender mercy has done just that. He has given away Christmas, once and for all eternity.

How Great A Cost

for Fr. Thomas Hickey

It was the Roaring Twenties, and life was full of promise for John Griffith. Griffith loved to travel, and he dreamed of visiting faraway lands with exotic names, far from his Midwestern home.

Before he could pursue his dreams, however, the stock market crash of 1929 ushered in the Great Depression. Like so many others, John Griffith and his family packed up their few possessions and headed east in search of work.

Griffith found a job in Missouri, controlling one of the huge railroad bridges that spanned the Mississippi River. Day after day he sat in the control room and worked the enormous gears that raised the bridge, allowing barges and ships to pass below. Each passing vessel was a bitter reminder of the travel he had given up and the dreams he had lost.

One day in 1937, John Griffith brought his 8-year-old son, Greg, to work with him. Greg delighted in the enormous cogs in the gearbox that raised and lowered the bridge. He thought his father must be the most powerful man in the world to control such a bridge.

The morning passed quickly. At noon, Griffith elevated the bridge to allow scheduled ships to pass through. He and his son were free until 1 p.m., when the bridge had to be lowered for the Memphis Express passenger train to cross the river.

Father and son scooped up their lunch sacks, edged across the narrow catwalk, and settled into the observation deck that jutted over the Mississippi River. They dangled their legs and watched the great passing ships, imagining where they might be headed.

Griffith was jerked out of his reverie by the shrill whistle of an oncoming train. Glancing at his watch, he was alarmed to read 1:07 – scarcely enough time to race to the control room and lower the bridge.

Instructing his son to stay in place, Griffith ran up the catwalk and climbed the steel ladder to the control room. He scanned the river for nearby ships, then glanced beneath the bridge for obstacles.

To his horror, Griffith saw that his son had slipped off the catwalk into the gearbox. His leg was lodged between the teeth of two giant cogs and was bleeding profusely. The child could not break free.

John Griffith wanted to run down to the gearbox with a rope, pull his son to safety, then climb back to the control room and press the heavy lever to lower the bridge for the oncoming train.

But he knew his desperate plan was hopeless. The train was bearing down at tremendous speed, and his son was too far below to be reached in time. Griffith was faced with an impossible choice: save his son and watch as 400 train passengers were hurled to certain death in the river below, or lower the drawbridge so the train could cross, but crush his son's small body.

The decision was excruciating, but he knew what he must do. Griffith buried his face in his arm and pressed down hard on the lever. The grinding of the bridge drowned the cries of his son. Seconds later, the Memphis Express thundered across the bridge, its occupants unaware that their safety had been secured at the cost of a man's only son.

John Griffith looked through the windows of the train as it sped past. Businessmen perused newspapers. Ladies chatted as they sipped tea. A conductor was checking his watch. A child was eating ice cream.

No one looked his way. Griffith wanted to scream, "What's the matter with you people? Don't you care? Don't you know I've sacrificed my son for you?"

But no one noticed him, and no one seemed to care as the train disappeared into the horizon.

****

This true story is an echo of Jesus' sacrifice for us, except that Jesus' death was not an accident. God intentionally gave up His Son for us.

Do we care?

Blip

for Benjamin

Moses was nearing the end of his long life. As he stood on the brink of the Promised Land, he begged the children of Israel to follow God's laws, which lead to eternal life. "I have set before you life and death, blessing and curse," Moses pleaded. "Therefore, choose life."

Choose life. It sounds pretty simple. I mean, who doesn't want life?

It may be simple, but that doesn't mean it's easy.

Think about it. Adoption may be the best solution for a teenage pregnancy, but it's certainly not easy – not when you're the one who is alone and confused and terrified of breaking the news to your parents. Chastity sounds simple too, but not in a world of pornography and 'safe sex,' of violence and chat rooms and hooking up.

Choosing life has never been easy. But God calls us to do it anyway.

A long time ago there was a lady in Hartford who chose life, and her decision changed my world forever.

It was a rainy spring morning when a young woman arrived at the hospital ultrasound lab. She already had two small children and she was pregnant again. At least, she used to be pregnant. She was pretty sure she had miscarried this new child. The doctor couldn't find a heartbeat and a previous ultrasound had revealed no sign of life.

The doctor had sent the woman for this follow-up test just to be sure, before scheduling her for post-miscarriage surgery. The woman arrived alone, distracted, and afraid. Her gaze kept sweeping across the ultrasound monitor in hopes of seeing her baby, but no baby appeared. The technician searched for a long time.

After what seemed an eternity, the young woman's fears were confirmed. There on the screen was the image of her lifeless child. Choking back tears, the young mother slumped back on the table. The doctor expressed his condolences and left the woman to her grief.

Her baby was dead – this child whom she loved even though she had never cradled him in her arms, never whispered his name. She turned away and wept, feeling more alone than ever. The rain drizzled against the window.

After a long while – or was it only a moment? - she realized that the technician had resumed the ultrasound. It made no sense. Hadn't the technician found what she was looking for?

"What are you doing?" the mother asked dully.

"Oh, I'm just looking a little more," the technician replied.

The mother didn't understand. What could the ultrasound show that could make any difference now? She stared blankly out the window, beyond the sanitized smell

21

and the hospital walls. She thought about her tiny son whose fingers would never curl around her own. There wouldn't even be a grave to mark his existence.

Suddenly the technician gasped. "Look at the monitor," she said quietly. "Do you see that blip?"

The young mother turned to look. There, in a sea of static, was a tiny *blip-blip-blip-blip* on the screen. "What is it?" the mother asked, afraid to hope.

"It's a heartbeat," the technician whispered. "It's your baby's heartbeat."

The mother was confused. "But my baby is dead. I saw him."

"Yes, he is," the technician explained gently, "and I am so sorry. But this is a second baby, and this one looks awesome."

And so she is awesome. Months later, that *blip-blip-blip* was born amidst much celebration, down the hall from the place where her life nearly ended. The baby was given the name Tierney.

I was that young mother. Tierney is alive today because the technician chose life. She was criticized for making other patients wait so long for their ultrasounds, but she was unwilling to end her search until she was absolutely certain about whether life existed. Why? Because life is awesome.

"I have set before you life and death, blessing and curse," God speaks to us tenderly. "Choose life."

Please.

The Voice of the Holy Spirit

for Craig and Liz Schantz, who are lights in the darkness

I met Caroline when she was a senior in high school. I was newly married and had begun working with the youth of the parish. Caroline quickly became one of my favorites.

Caroline and I stayed in touch after she graduated. She was a young woman of tremendous faith with a deep desire for marriage and children. More than anything, Caroline yearned for a devout Catholic man with whom she could share her life on a spiritual level. She was not willing to compromise on this, even if it meant waiting a long time.

She waited a long time.

Caroline and I hadn't seen each other for a while when we found ourselves sitting in adjacent pews at the wedding of a mutual friend. The outdoor reception was leisurely and relaxed, giving us plenty of time to catch up. After a few minutes, Caroline leaned close and whispered, "May I ask your advice about something important?"

She confided that she'd been seeing a man for about six months – a wonderful, devout Catholic man who was a bit older than she was. David was everything she had ever wanted in a husband, and she was falling in love with him.

The problem was that David was divorced, and while he had applied for an annulment, it had not yet been granted. But, Caroline stressed, "the annulment is just a piece of paper." She went on to explain that David had stayed in his troubled marriage for years after his wife had asked for a divorce. He'd begged her to reconsider and insisted on joint counseling, but the marriage broke up nevertheless. After the divorce, David had waited several more years before pursuing an annulment because he still held out hope for reconciliation. "He's very committed to marriage," Caroline insisted. "It's not as if he bolted at the first sign of trouble."

Caroline had a nagging concern about dating David, however, so she sought out my opinion on the matter.

I've never been fast on my feet. I stumbled for words, encouraging her to be cautious and to take things slowly . . . something brilliant like that.

The problem was that my advice was wrong.

For days thereafter, I ruminated over Caroline's situation. Gradually I homed in on the central issue: Caroline was dating a married man.

David sounded wonderful. He'd probably make a great husband. But until his annulment was granted, he was married. And if he was married, Caroline had no business dating him.

I decided to send a handwritten letter to Caroline. I wrote that I loved her dearly and wanted to clarify the muddy advice I'd offered in person. Then, in a compassionate and straightforward manner, I said that until an annulment was granted, David remained married, and hence they should not be dating.

I also addressed the issue of an annulment being "just" a piece of paper. The same might be said of the deed to a house, I wrote, or adoption papers, or a will. And yet these pieces of paper change the very fabric of our lives. Talk to a person who was imprisoned in a Nazi death camp, and ask if his or her release decree means anything. A piece of paper can be the difference between life and death, marriage and divorce, poverty and wealth. In David's case, it meant that David was married, and hence was not free to date anyone else.

I held my letter for several days. Then, with much prayer, I mailed it. And I waited.

Days went by. A week. Just as I was starting to panic, Caroline called me with a remarkable story.

When she had read my letter, Caroline realized immediately that I'd spoken the truth; in fact, it was the very truth she'd been trying to avoid. She felt an odd sense of relief as she acknowledged it.

With much trepidation, Caroline called David to tell him that she wanted to discuss something important with him. He was having dinner with an old friend that evening so they arranged to see each other afterwards.

When Caroline arrived at David's apartment, he met her with a nervous hug. "I need to tell you something," David blurted out before Caroline could say anything. "I had dinner tonight with my old friend, Zach Turner. Zach told me something I did not want to hear; he said you and I should not be dating until my annulment is granted. He's right, Caroline. I'm so sorry, but we have to stop seeing each other."

Caroline was speechless. When she regained her composure, she told David that she, too, had heard from an old friend with the same message. Both friends had loved them enough to speak the truth.

David and Caroline stopped seeing each other. It was excruciating. Seven months later, David received the news that his annulment had been granted.

Today, David and Caroline are married with two young children. Some things are worth the wait.

From the Snare of Death

for Mary-Jane Zocco, who cares for all

"Karen, do you know where you are? Do you know you had a transplant?"

These were the first words Karen Woodbury heard on Jan. 5, 1992 when she awoke from a coma. A liver transplant had saved her from the edge of death where she had teetered for weeks.

In the spring of 1991, Karen Woodbury developed a fungal infection in her index finger. A doctor eventually prescribed Nizoral, a potent drug with potential for serious side effects including liver damage.

A few months later Karen's bilirubin count, the measure of liver function, began to skyrocket. Within days it was more than 20 times normal.

In the early hours of Nov. 20, Karen Woodbury collapsed in her home. Her daughter Alison was asleep in the crib but 4-year-old Brian heard his mother's cries. He brought Karen the mobile phone, covered her with his Teenage Mutant Ninja Turtle blanket, and curled up with her on the bathroom floor to await the paramedics.

Karen was hospitalized for two and a half months in

liver failure. Surgeons first broached the subject of a liver transplant around Thanksgiving but Karen threw them out of her hospital room. "I don't want them in my room again!" she insisted. "They're knife-happy; they just want to take out my liver."

In December surgeons approached Karen about a liver that had become available for transplant. Still not realizing how sick she was, Karen declined. "You guys are all knife-happy!" she again charged. "I'm going to get better."

Meanwhile her liver function continued to deteriorate. Karen developed encephalopathy, a dangerous inflammation of the brain as toxins built up, impairing her ability to think.

In order to assess brain function, Karen's doctors made her perform mental exercises each day. "In the beginning I thought it was so ridiculous, doing connect-the-dots and counting backwards," she explains. "But every day it was harder to remember what came after 27. There was an emptiness in my brain. The day after I turned down the liver, I realized that I couldn't count backwards anymore." That day, Karen Woodbury agreed to be added to the transplant list.

Karen's husband later told her, "One day you thought you were 25 [years old]; the next day you'd be 45. You never knew how many kids you had."

"I don't remember that," Karen says now. "I do remember arguing with my doctor that Mario Cuomo was the president."

After drifting in and out of consciousness for much of December, Karen sank into a coma on Christmas Day,

1991. "At the very end, my kidneys shut down, I was on dialysis, my pancreas shut down, and they were concerned about hemorrhaging in my brain," Karen explains. She was given the Sacrament of the Sick, and the family found itself in the uncomfortable position of awaiting someone else's tragedy to provide a liver for Karen.

On January 3, 1992, Karen Woodbury received that liver from a 16-year-old girl who had been thrown from a horse and became brain dead.

During that period, Karen remembers an extremely bright light, and voices trying to get her attention. When she was near the light, she felt tremendous calm and peace. In contrast, the voices pulled her away from the light toward pain and reality.

Karen sensed that she had a choice to make. "If I agreed to hear the voices, I'd have to take the pain and suffering and it would mean going away from the light. If I took the route to the light, I would not see my family. It was a difficult choice."

Karen chose to hear the voices. The first voice she heard said, "Karen, do you know where you are? Do you know you had a transplant?"

It was Jan. 5, 1992, two days after the grueling 17-hour liver transplant surgery.

Recovery was long. "The mental fogginess wears off really slowly. I had so much poison accumulated," Karen explains. "I couldn't read; I couldn't focus. I couldn't put on the TV because I couldn't figure out the remote control."

Friends provided child care, meals, and moral support during the long ordeal. One friend decorated the house for Christmas; others bought Christmas gifts and filled the stockings for the children. Neighbors rushed to the hospital during the night of January 2 in order to donate plasma when a critical shortage endangered the transplant surgery scheduled the following morning. Friends gave daily back massages to ease Karen's severe pain from her being so long in bed.

To thank all who helped, the Woodburys threw a Celebration of Life party in July, 1992, six months after the surgery. "This party is for you, in your honor," they told the guests. Two hundred people came.

"It's ironic," Karen muses now. "For 35 years, I wanted more, more, more. For my next 35, I'll appreciate my husband, my children. It makes me think how blessed I am."

Entertaining Angels Unaware

for Angelique

New Year's day was unusual that year. After packing for my upcoming hospital stay and trying to explain to a 2-year-old how babies get born, my husband Peter and I resumed spirited negotiations on a a boy's name. We had 36 hours before this child's arrival, and I did not want the birth announcement to read, "Baby Cram." Neither did Peter, but that was our only point of agreement.

I wanted to name the baby James or Benjamin. Peter preferred Samuel, and he was especially fond the of nickname, 'Buttons.'

"Are you telling me that my choices are Sam Cram or Buttons?" I asked with incredulity. "Let's just hope it's a girl."

A day and a half later, we welcomed a tiny but beautiful infant daughter, Elizabeth Tierney Cram. We rocked her and sang to her in the delivery room as she fell asleep in Daddy's arms. All too soon, however, a staff member whisked her away to an incubator. The baby was borderline premature and rather thin, so she was having a hard time staying warm.

Peter left to make phone calls, and I was wheeled to my hospital room. And then I waited.

Each time my nurse came within view, I asked for my baby. "She needs more time to warm up," the nurse would reply. A new nurse came on duty mid-afternoon but she, too, insisted that the baby needed to remain in the nursery.

By 9:00 that evening, I was in tears. "I just want to hold my baby," I sobbed to Peter, who had been equally unsuccessful getting Tierney released from the hospital nursery.

That's when an unfamiliar nurse strode into my room. She couldn't have been more than 4'9" high and almost as wide, with a mop of salt and pepper curls, and a thick Irish brogue.

"And how are you tonight, m'lady?" she asked with genuine mirth.

"They won't give me my baby!" I cried. "I just want my baby!"

"What?" the nurse bellowed. "That baby needs her mama! This mama needs her baby! I'm going to tell those people to hand over your baby!" And with that, she stormed out of the room.

Peter and I looked at each other in curious disbelief. A moment later, we heard the familiar *rattle-rattle-rattle* of bassinet wheels in the corridor.

Sure enough, our Irish nurse returned with a tiny, wide-eyed bundle rolled up tight in a pink blanket.

"How did you convince them?" I asked, incredulous.

"I just marched m'self down to the nursery and told those people, 'That baby needs her mama! That mama needs her baby!'"

"Thank you," I sputtered as she departed, leaving us alone with our beautiful daughter.

Moments later, my regular nurse entered the room. Her eyes immediately fell on the newborn cradled in my arms.

"Who brought that baby in here?" she demanded with an accusatory tone. Peter and I described the Irish nurse with salt and pepper hair. Without lingering to check on me, the maternity nurse turned on her heels and disappeared.

A few minutes later she returned, asking us to repeat the description of the offending nurse. Again we described her as short and plump with a mop of curly hair and a strong Irish brogue.

"That's impossible," the nurse insisted. "No one by that description works at this hospital, nor has there ever been such a nurse."

We never saw the Irish nurse again.

Several months later, Peter reminded me of the incident. Only then did he suggest an unusual possibility: perhaps our Irish nurse was an angel in disguise. No one had ever seen her before, no one in the hospital knew her, and she was never seen again.

Hey, it's possible. Throughout Scripture, God sent angels to announce news, guide people to safety, and provide for the needs of His children. It was an angel who protected Daniel in the lions' den. An angel visited young Mary with the news that she was to become the mother of the Savior. Angels guarded Jesus' empty tomb, and it was an angel who protected the Apostle Paul as he traveled to

Rome.

There is mystery surrounding angels, but we do know that they are entirely distinct from humans. People do not morph into angels after death, any more than a rhododendron turns into a fire hydrant. Angels are God's messengers; people are God's children.

I still wonder about my Irish nurse. And if indeed she was an angel, it seems fitting that she would answer the cries of a mother for her newborn child.

"Do not neglect to show hospitality to strangers, for thereby some have entertained angels unawares." Heb. 13:2

Corrie ten Boom

for the Doty sisters

The year was 1942, and Holland was under Nazi occupation. The elderly Casper ten Boom and his middle-aged daughters were leading quiet lives as watchmakers until Jewish neighbors began disappearing.

One night after curfew, a terrified Jewish woman arrived at the door of the ten Boom shop. The woman's husband had just been arrested, her son was in hiding, and she was afraid to return home for fear of arrest. She'd heard that the Christian ten Boom family had helped a Jewish neighbor, and she didn't know where else to turn. Casper ten Boom kindly assured her, "In this household, God's people are always welcome."

Thus began a steady stream of frightened Jews seeking refuge. At first, Betsie and Corrie ten Boom housed the visitors in their extra rooms, but they quickly ran out of space.

More pressing was the matter of food. Every non-Jewish Dutch person was issued a ration card, but Jews received no ration cards, and food was scarce due to wartime shortages. For a while, Corrie and Betsie shuttled

Jews to safe houses, or to outlying farms where food was not as scarce. After a while, however, even farms were full.

Corrie begged God to provide a solution. Almost immediately, she recalled a Dutch man who worked at the local ration card office. She visited the man's home unannounced one evening and, at great risk, stated that she needed illegal ration cards. When he asked how many, she opened her mouth to say, 'Five.' "But," Corrie wrote later, "the number that unexpectedly and astonishingly came out instead was 'one hundred.'"

Over the next two years, the ten Booms developed contacts across Holland, working with members of the Dutch Resistance to hide as many as 600 Jews. Underground sympathizers built a secret room on the top floor of the ten Boom home, hidden behind a false wall. A buzzer was installed to give warning of a raid.

But their actions placed them in constant danger. Once, a Nazi officer jeeringly asked Casper ten Boom if he knew he could die for helping Jews. The elderly watchmaker replied, "It would be an honor to give my life for God's ancient people." In the end, he did.

Early in 1944, the Nazis raided the watch shop and arrested the ten Booms. The Gestapo ransacked the house but never found the secret room where six Jews crouched in terrified silence. Resistance workers were able to liberate the refugees two days later.

Casper ten Boom died after only 10 days in captivity. Corrie and Betsie were shuttled to three different prisons, the last being the infamous Ravensbruck Concentration Camp where they saw unimaginable horrors.

Life in the camp was nearly unbearable, with

cramped barracks that were so foul and flea-infested that Corrie wondered aloud why God had created fleas. Corrie and Betsie led nightly prayer meetings and Bible studies, sharing Jesus' love with fellow prisoners who were hungry for hope. Corrie marveled that these meetings were never raided by guards. Gradually she realized why the guards refused to enter the barracks: fleas. Corrie was forced to thank God for the fleas.

On Christmas Day 1944, Corrie ten Boom's beloved sister Betsie died at Ravensbruck Prison. A few days later, Corrie was released. She later learned that her release was the result of a clerical error, and that all women prisoners her age were put to death a week after she was set free.

It was two years after the war when Corrie spotted him – a balding, heavyset man who greeted Corrie after her speech about God's forgiveness and healing. Instantly, Corrie recognized him as the cruel guard at Ravensbruck who had been instrumental in Betsie's death.

The man admitted that he'd been at Ravensbruck but explained that in the years since, he had opened his heart to Jesus. "I know that God has forgiven me for the cruel things I did there, but I would like to hear it from your lips, as well, Fraulein," he said, extending his hand. "Will you forgive me?"

Corrie stood there in shock. She hated this man, this horrible guard who had tortured people for fun.

And yet, Corrie knew that she must forgive him, for it was a condition placed on her own forgiveness.

"Jesus, help me!" she cried out silently to God.

Mechanically, without feeling, Corrie took the man's hand and uttered the words, "I forgive you, brother." And as she did so, God began to melt the ice in her heart.

Later, Corrie wrote, "For a long moment we grasped each other's hands, the former guard and the former prisoner. I had never known God's love so intensely as I did then."

"If you forgive men their trespasses, your heavenly Father also will forgive you; but if you do not forgive men their trespasses, neither will your Father forgive your trespasses." Matt. 6:14-15

Corrie ten Boom tells her story in her book, *The Hiding Place.*

The Lost Sheep

for Andrew

Susannah joined our family on Mother's Day, 1989. She bears little resemblance to our other children, however, because she is not made of flesh and bone. Susannah is our daughter Tierney's beloved stuffed bunny.

Susannah arrived fat and bunchy, as pure and clean as the baby whose baptism was being celebrated that day. Before long, her rugged good looks and firm definition gave way to a lumpy body the color of mottled dirt, and a right paw that was rubbed bald. They were inseparable – Tierney and that lump of fur that, in her baby voice, she called, "my Shada."

By 18 months of age Tierney's favorite place of adventure was the laundry room, with Susannah in tow, of course. No campaign to keep the door closed succeeded in thwarting Tierney's one-woman mission to create havoc. She loved to remove clumps of dryer lint from the wastebasket, gently shred them, then plop them into the toilet. Whenever I overheard, "Dirty. Dirty," I knew our intrepid toddler had broken into the laundry room again and needed to be retrieved. Fast.

It didn't take long for Tierney to discover that Susannah made a far better projectile than lint balls. Soon thereafter I found Tierney clinging to a dripping Susannah, cheerfully muttering, "Dirty, dirty."

Tierney pointed to the wet spot on the rug and announced with glee, "Uh-oh." Susannah had taken an unauthorized swim in the toilet. I sternly told Tierney that we don't put bunnies in the toilet, then plopped the dripping creature into the washing machine.

Tierney was devastated. She stood in front of the washer and sobbed, "Shada! My Shada!" for the entire duration of the wash and dry cycles.

After what seemed an interminable wait, I handed a clean, dry Susannah to her anxious friend. But as soon as I turned my back I heard a distinct *splash!* and a little voice mumbling, "Uh-oh. Dirty. Dirty."

That same year Susannah got lost at Bradley International Airport as we raced to surprise my husband at the gate. We retraced our steps but Susannah had vanished. It was out of the question to abandon her 30 miles from home so I made my way to the lost and found, located in the State Police barracks above the airport terminal. The dispatcher looked at me as if I were out of my mind as I explained the urgency in locating a tattered stuffed bunny. "Can't you just buy another one?" he asked, incredulous.

"Another *Susannah*?" I gasped. "With a paw rubbed bald, and a sailor hat that's frayed behind the ear, and matted fur in the shape of Tierney's face? I don't think so."

He just shook his head and filed the report.

Once again Tierney and Susannah were eventually reunited, and several happy years followed. But the day finally arrived when Susannah simply vanished. It had been a busy afternoon with a young family so Susannah's absence was not noted until bedtime. We looked everywhere for her, turning the house upside down and searching the neighborhood in torrential rain, without success. Poor Tierney was heartbroken.

For days Tierney wandered around the house calling Susannah's name. When Susannah did not respond, Tierney would sink into her tiny rocking chair and sob. "Doesn't God know where's my Shada?" Tierney would ask with pitiful eyes. "Then why doesn't He tell us?"

I had no reply.

The days stretched into weeks. That's when she grew to love the story of the lost sheep. A farmer has 100 sheep, and when one wanders off, the farmer searches until he finds it. Then he throws a big party to celebrate.

One day Tierney asked, "Why did the farmer go after the sheep? He still had all those other sheeps."

I asked if she thought we'd look for her if she got lost. After all, we'd still have three kids left.

She was shocked and shouted, "Yes! Because you love me!" Her eyes glistened as we assured her that we'd never, ever stop looking until we found her.

"Then would we have a party?" she pressed. "A big party? With cake?"

And so it was that a party was held for a lumpy stuffed bunny who was found after weeks deep inside a closet. Susannah even shared her cake with Tierney, "because Susannah isn't too hungry tonight."

And now, one four-year-old understands something of God's great love and the lengths to which He goes to reach us, like torrential rain, or birth in a cold Bethlehem stable.

A Time to Live

for Drs. Jack Monaco and Clark O'Brien

The morning of July 31 dawned like any other, except that this day I was actually awake to see the sunrise. While the children and my father-in-law slept, my husband and I silently gathered our things and slipped into the gray dawn for the drive to the hospital that we had been planning for nine months. The nursery was ready, the birth announcements were addressed, and Peter had a list of family and friends to call when James Allen or Louise Victoria had his or her appearance.

My textbook pregnancy led into a smooth, rapid labor. I even got the epidural I had so fervently wanted. But moments before birth, something went terribly wrong: I suffered a rare Amniotic Fluid Embolism that left me struggling for survival on the delivery table.

In rapid succession the baby was born, I was rushed into surgery, transfusions began, and Peter was left to ponder, and panic, and pray. He could hear terrifying snippets of conversation in the corridor: "Hurry! . . . Extremely critical . . . Prep more blood . . . There's not enough time left . . . "

When the first procedure failed to stem the collapse of my clotting system, the surgeon swiftly briefed Peter and secured his permission to perform an emergency hysterectomy on me. The doctor hurried out of the room, then turned back and quietly said, "You know we'll do everything we can, Peter, but I don't think we can save her."

And he was gone.

Frightened and alone in the delivery room, Peter called our parish priest. The priest placed a quick call to the first person on our parish prayer chain, then left for the hospital.

I have a funny picture in my mind of this dear priest praying desperately for my life while breaking every traffic law in the state of Connecticut. Driving along the interstate en route to the hospital, the priest had a vision of the woman who was hemorrhaging, reaching out to touch the hem of Jesus' garment. It was just like the story in the Gospel of Mark: as soon as the woman touched Jesus' robe, she was healed, and Jesus realized that power had gone out from Him. The woman sheepishly admitted that she was the person who had touched Him; Jesus told her to go in peace, healed of her disease.

As the vision came to an end, the woman turned so the priest could see her face, and the woman had my face. At that moment, our priest knew that I had been healed. The clock on the dashboard read 6:27 p.m.

Meanwhile, the prayer chain coordinator returned home to find a message detailing my situation. She made several quick calls to relay the message, then set to prayer. For a long time she implored God to spare my life and heal me. "She has a husband and four tiny children, Lord," the woman cried. "That baby has never looked into her mother's eyes, never heard the sounds of her mother's laughter. Please, Lord, spare Reg's life."

Suddenly from near despair, the woman was overwhelmed with a sense of peace about my condition. She glanced at her watched and noted the time: 6:27.

Back at the hospital, eight doctors and every available nurse were waging a losing battle against an extraordinary crisis, a rare type of embolism that kills 86% of its victims, usually within minutes. The situation was so critical that they did not scrub for surgery. Despite the transfusion of 25 units of blood, my clotting factor continued to plummet during surgery, from 750 and 600 . . . 420 . . . 190 . . . 55 . . . It got down to 12, which meant that I had gone into DIC, a complete collapse of my clotting system. Patients in DIC die.

The surgeon later explained that he was totally unprepared for my impending death. He had entered obstetrics because it was happy medicine and he did not expect a healthy 34-year-old woman to die on his operating table. Only a short while earlier we had been joking about naming the baby after him if he could shorten my labor.

When the surgeon realized that I was going to die, he began to steel himself against the devastating scene in front of him. He knew that within the next minute, he would have to declare the time of death, pull up the sheet, and turn off the light. Then he'd make the long walk down the corridor to tell Peter that he was sorry, that he had done everything he could, but that his wife was dead.

As the doctor braced himself for this certain outcome, I began to revive. My pulse strengthened, the clotting factor started to rise, and the doctor realized that his desperate prayers for God's intervention had been answered.

He glanced at the clock on the operating room wall. It was 6:27.

Thanks Giving

for Pandy Dumas Wohler

During the noisy years when our children were small, our favorite summer destination was the pool down the street. We loved the water slide and swimming lessons and swings, but most of all, we loved Tony.

Tony was our favorite lifeguard and swim coach with a remarkable knack for kids. He spent one entire summer coaxing our shy toddler into the pool, proudly displaying her progress at summer's end when she jumped off the diving board into his arms. After that, she'd often run to him giggling, "You're my Tony Bologna," as he scooped her up and swung her in the air.

During Tony's last summer, 9-year-old Skip complained to anyone who would listen that he was the only kid in America whose mom wouldn't let him see the new PG-13 *Jurassic Park* movie. One day Tony beckoned Skip with a secretive air and whispered something to the wide-eyed child. Afterward Skip informed us, "Tony saw *Jurassic Park* last night and it was so scary that he practically had nightmares. He says I definitely shouldn't see it." Skip never asked again. I almost kissed Tony.

So we were devastated a month later when Tony was killed in Moscow where he had gone to study. He left a hole that has never been filled, and a legacy that still inspires the kids whose lives he touched. Summer after summer Tony showed scores of impressionable kids that kindness is cool and that teenagers can make a difference in their corner of the world.

I wonder if I ever thanked him for that.

Why is it that we don't thank people more? I don't mean the quick thank-you we toss to the sales clerk, or the grudging thanks a teenager is required to mumble when Grandma gives him socks for his birthday. I mean heartfelt appreciation, the kind when we genuinely express to another person how much he means to us, and why.

Most of us don't do this very often. Let's face it – it feels awkward until we get used to it. To ward off guilt, we convince ourselves that the other person already knows how we feel. Besides, there's always tomorrow.

But sometimes tomorrow doesn't come. A sudden heart attack or a tragic accident, and the chance is gone forever. So we tell the next-of-kin how much their loved one meant to us, and quietly resolve to not take people, or life, for granted again. Then, imperceptibly, we return to our old ways. Until the next tragedy.

Even Jesus appreciated the value of expressing our thanks. After healing 10 lepers, Jesus commended the only one who returned to thank Him. Surely the other nine were grateful as well, but to Jesus, it was important to actually say so.

I once wrote a note to a physician who was

instrumental in saving my life. I told him that a good surgeon is like having 'mad money' on a date: you hope you never need it but if you do, you're *really* glad to have it. I wrote that I was profoundly grateful, and that saving a life is a precious thing I did not take for granted just because it was supposed to be his job.

I later learned that the doctor carried my note in his pocket for months. Once again I was reminded how much a simple expression of thanks can mean.

I wish I had kept remembering.

At swimming championships during Tony's last summer, our competitive 9-year-old was convinced that he was a top finisher in breast stroke. When the standings were posted, however, Skip found himself in sixth place. Fighting back tears, he sought out his swim coach.

Tony knelt down to look Skip in the eye, and as he explained the scoring system, Skip began to grin. "Tony says I'm the sixth-best breast stroker in the whole league, and I'm only 9!" Skip proudly announced to us afterwards.

I left the pool that day with a deep affection for Tony, whose gentle way made a child feel like a giant.

I just wish I had told him so.

Ice Puddle

for my father, whose love was great and tender

Okay, so it wasn't the smartest thing I ever did to get lost in a wintry forest with no food, no phone, and two tiny kids. How was I supposed to know the map was wrong?

Fine. I'll tell the story; just don't call me stupid. In my house, 'stupid' is a swear word.

It was a cloudy December morning and our younger children had just finished watching 'Sesame Street.' I had to mail a package so I grabbed our jackets, strapped the girls into their car seats, and proceeded to the post office.

I was curious about an old road I'd seen on a local map so afterwards we headed to the rural outskirts of town. The girls, ages 3 and 1, chattered happily in the back seat. The pine trees glistened with new fallen snow and the country road was covered with several inches of slushy ice. We drove past old farmhouses and apple orchards, then into a winter wonderland. The houses disappeared behind us as we continued through the sparkling woods.

I should have noticed that the forest was deeper than the map indicated; in fact, we should have emerged on the other side after a mile or two. Instead, we had become surrounded by thick woods that tightly hemmed the road. The road itself had narrowed so much that it was scarcely passable and it banked steeply down to icy swamps and streams. Under the snow the road was no longer paved. It began to occur to me that we might be in trouble.

Three-year-old Tierney piped up in the back seat. "Where're we goin', Mama? Are we getting' lost?" I didn't dare answer. The road had become too narrow to turn around, and the slightest mistake in backing up would have rolled us into the icy swamp below. My only choice was to continue deeper into the forest until we emerged on the other side or the path widened enough to turn around.

"Please help us, Lord," I silently prayed. "Keep these dear ones safe, and protect them from my foolishness." This was no longer a fun adventure. I was scared.

After another mile we came to a small clearing. Breathing a sigh of thanks, I carefully planned a three-point turn where the ground was most secure. I made a sharp turn left, straightened the wheel, put the van into reverse, and promptly spun my tires in the deep icy slush. Even my practiced winter driving was not able to dislodge that minivan. We were stuck.

There I was, deep in the forest with two babies, no food or water, and minimal winter clothing. Hey, I said it wasn't the smartest thing I ever did.

I put the baby into the infant backpack that I always kept in the trunk. I cinched her hood and pulled the cuffs over her tiny hands. She was perfectly happy.

We found an abandoned hat under Tierney's seat (thank you, Lord). I wedged her tattered stuffed bunny inside her jacket (with head protruding so the bunny could breathe), took her hand, and explained that we would hike out until we found someone to help us. I grimaced at the thought of admitting to some stranger that I'd been so stupid. Oh right, we don't say stupid. So foolish.

To combat our fear, Tierney and I sang. We belted out "The Itsy Bitsy Spider," "Jesus Loves Me" and "The Backwards CBA." We sang about how God is always watching over us, and about a guy who got stuck on the subway because he didn't have a nickel to get off. As we sang, our fear dissolved.

Eventually we came upon a farmhouse in the distance. The inhabitants 'happened' to be home that morning and, like messengers from God, their help was generous and immediate. They gave snacks to the children, let me use the telephone to arrange a ride home, and asked for details about my van.

"I've got a truck," mentioned the gentleman. "The guy across the street is home and together we could tow your van out of the woods."

I was flabbergasted by his generosity. In the end, the three adults were able to rock the van out of the slush and drive it safely back to civilization. After many and profuse thanks, the girls and I headed home.

Sitting in our warm kitchen an hour later as the baby banged pots and pans, Tierney said with a mischievous grin, "That was a stupid idea, Mama. I'm not s'posed to say 'stupid,' but that was a stupid idea."

Yes it was. And yet God, in His great and tender love, cared for us even when we shouldn't have been in that situation in the first place. Great and tender is the Father's love.

To Kneel Before the Savior

for Alexandra Kravontka

When we first set up our hardy wooden creche many years ago, we began finding it surrounded by creatures not mentioned in Luke Chapter 2. Meredith, then 2½, loved to intermingle three plastic dinosaurs amidst the sheep, oxen and camels. She also kept stealing the Baby Jesus and hiding him at the bottom of her Christmas stocking.

Not to be outdone, 4-year-old Skip assembled hoards of tiny rubber muscle men in order to dive-bomb the stable. Sometimes his stuffed gorilla kept guard.

The following July they begged to set it up again. Why not? The story is for always, not just Christmas day. This time Skip brought out his G.I. Joe attack jet. It was a gift from a friend who, knowing our dislike of toy guys, thoughtfully gave him instead a war plane armed with 16 miniature bombs. Skip insisted that he was not bombing the Holy Family; he was protecting Jesus from bad guys.

For a long time the stable was home to Teenage Mutant Ninja Turtles, followed by Barney dolls, Barbie dolls, and army guys. One year the sheep kept disappearing as young Tierney attempted to gum them to death. Another offspring, who shall remain nameless, still enjoys looping the shepherds' crooks over the roof of the stable so they can scale the walls like technical rock climbers. There's also a running dispute as to whether the sheep should be neatly lined up in a row, or clustered en masse like children at recess. Each day holds a new adventure.

But some confusion arose during the early years. It began quite innocently when we purchased the original stable. It came with animals, wise men and Baby Jesus but no parents or shepherds. (It was on sale.) Our kids were understandably upset that the poor Baby was left to fend for Himself so we designated the wise men as Mary, Joseph and a friend. It seemed to satisfy them.

Several years later we received a beautiful handmade set from my sister Ginny, mother of six and artistic queen of Texas. Combined, they make a spectacular Nativity scene. We now have a real Mary and Joseph, six wise men, two shepherds, plenty of bleating sheep, and one big problem: we have twin Baby Jesuses.

We knew our 3-year-old was confused when she told her friend that Christmas is a birthday party for the Jesus twins. We tried explaining that there is really only one Jesus, and Meredith told her that it was sort of like having two different Barbie dolls. Our daughter was unconvinced.

Many years have passed since we became the only family in town with Jesus twins. Fortunately the time finally arrived when the confusion dissipated. "Christmas is coming soon!" our youngest child squealed a few winters ago. "That means we all get presents because it's Jesus' birfday! And we get to sing Happy Birfday to Jesus, too!"

"But Torrie, there's only one Jesus, you know," 6-year-old Tierney instructed with an air of superiority. "Don't get confused just because we have two of them in our living room."

"Everybody knows that!" Torrie replied in disgust.

Throughout it all we have reveled in the sight of our children celebrating the birth of the Savior. We are reminded that as a grown man, Jesus called out for the children to come to Him. And we stand in awe of a God who has showered His people with life, love, and most of all, His Son, to whom ultimately, every creature will bow.

Maybe even Teenage Mutant Ninja Turtles.

A First Communion

for Fr. John Gwozdz, who showed us the way

We celebrated a First Communion this week.

Not just any First Communion. This one marked the end of a family journey that began years ago, a journey fraught with misconceptions, prejudice, and fear.

With this First Communion, our family has become Catholic.

My husband Peter and I spent our first 18 years of marriage in born-again churches. Gradually, Peter grew disturbed by the lack of ultimate authority on matters of faith and morals so, reluctantly, he began to look for a new church. Protestant, of course.

He looked at the Methodists. He studied the Lutherans, the Assemblies of God, and independent Bible churches. Finally he decided to take a quick look at the Catholics so that in good conscience, he could rule it out. He was certain it would be a simple process; no self-respecting evangelical would seriously consider the Catholic Church.

The first thing Peter did was to read the Catechism. The whole thing. That led him to the Early Church Fathers, the Desert Monastics, St. John of the Cross, Church encyclicals; you know, lightweight stuff. The problem was that he kept bumping into truth so he had to keep reading. He was confident that if he looked long enough, he'd find the loopholes.

Instead of loopholes, however, my husband discovered one, holy, catholic and apostolic Church founded by Jesus and handed down through the apostles. Just like the Catholic Church says.

Eventually I joined the search. We were horrified at the prospect of becoming Catholic, but from the outset we had promised God that we would follow wherever He led. Even if – *gulp* – He led us to that place. You know . . . the Catholic place.

In the meantime, family and friends mobilized. My mother and stepfather, bless their hearts, fasted and prayed for us every Friday for years. My sister and brother-in-law provided biblical and historical support for difficult issues like the papacy, Immaculate Conception, and prayers to saints. It was getting harder to escape.

On Pentecost Sunday, 1996, after three years of begging God to change His mind, Peter and I made the difficult decision to become Catholic. "Let's go home and I'll make pizza," I concluded glumly. "At least we'll have *something* to look forward to."

As our family of six settled into the pew at St. Paul Catholic Church in Glastonbury, Connecticut a few weeks later, I blinked back tears of despair. The place smelled funny. It looked funny. We stood when we were supposed to kneel, grumbled about the fussy babies, and plowed into "for thine is the kingdom and the power and the glory" at the end of the Our Father. It was an uncomfortable fit.

Gradually, however, we began to feel at home as we grew in our appreciation for the sacraments. More than anything, Peter and I fell in love with the Eucharist.

Remember that Protestants view communion as only a representation. As we slowly grasped the truth that Jesus is actually present in the Eucharist, it put into perspective all those persnickety issues about Catholic life. It really doesn't matter if the music sounds strange to our ears, or if Sunday's homily was dull, or if that lady behind me really should quiet her squirmy kid, because at 7:30 every morning, we can receive Jesus in the Eucharist.

This reality has changed our lives.

I began attending weekday Mass as often as possible, further deepening my hunger for the Eucharist. But when my car died, I could no longer make it to weekday Mass.

I lasted about ten days. "Babe," I pleaded with Peter when I'd reached my limit, "I am starving for the Eucharist; once a week on Sundays just isn't enough. Can we find a way for get me to mid-week Mass, even if it's just once?"

We put our heads together, and a few days later Peter dropped me off at our church. Mass was glorious. Then I walked home, six miles in torrential rain.

That's when I knew that the Real Presence of Christ in the Eucharist was changing my life.

It has changed our children as well. Young Tierney quickly developed a passionate love for the Eucharist, even though it was nearly a year after our arrival before she received her First Communion. Every night during that time she'd beg me, "Are you going to Mass tomorrow, Mom? Please, *please* may I come?"

So I was surprised when Tierney came to me in tears one evening about six weeks before her First Communion. "I don't think I can come to Mass with you anymore," she said. "Why not, sweetheart?" I asked. "It's too hard," she sobbed. "Jesus is right there in the room with me, and I can receive Him. It's just too hard."

The Real Presence of Christ in the Eucharist was changing our children as well.

One by one, each of the six of us has been received into the Catholic Church. This week our youngest child received her First Communion, officially signaling her reception into the Catholic Church and marking the conclusion of our long journey. What a journey it has been.

As Victoria received that precious Body and Blood, again I cried. But this time, they were tears of joy, and gratitude for God's goodness, and jubilation that we finally did it.

We followed where God had led. Even to that Catholic place.

John McKaig: Portrait of a Deacon

for Pat McKaig

"I was two hours, 45 minutes from being an April Fools joke," says John McKaig, a financial services consultant and permanent deacon in the Catholic Church.

Born March 31, 1943 in Providence, R.I., he settled in Connecticut at age 10 when his father was named chief of police in a town outside Hartford.

After graduation from high school, John went to work in a heat treat factory until longtime family friend Charlie Monaco offered him a job as a car salesman. Weighing only 125 pounds and painfully shy, Mr. McKaig looked at the floor as he replied, "Charlie, I can't even look anybody in the face. How can I sell cars?"

Mr. McKaig still remembers Charlie Monaco's response. "I'll teach you. As long as you're fair, you're honest, and you're moral, you can accomplish anything."

So Mr. McKaig began selling cars, and by age 21 he was a top salesman. "Charlie Monaco made all the difference in my life," he says now. "He took me out of a factory and he put a white shirt and tie on me. He gave me the keys to my future."

John met his wife at a beach party. Pat came from a devout Catholic family so John, an Episcopalian, converted to Catholicism. "My father-in-law did not want someone to marry his daughter who wasn't Catholic, especially if he was a used-car salesman," John laughs.

Nevertheless, God played no role in Mr. McKaig's life. "Money was my god," he says. "The only time I went to church was when my father-in-law was in town."

By age 28, John McKaig's life was a mess. He had a bleeding ulcer so severe that doctors planned to remove his stomach. He had become a drinker and a smoker, and was driving 70,000 miles a year as a salesman, seeing little of his wife and young son. But on Dec. 29, 1971, the day his daughter was born, Mr. McKaig took his last drink. It was the beginning of dramatic changes in his life.

The following week, Mr. McKaig found himself in the driveway of St. Paul Catholic Church in Glastonbury, Connecticut. For reasons he still does not understand, Mr. McKaig walked inside the empty church, knelt near the altar and looked up to the crucifix. At that moment, something inexplicable happened. "I felt as red as a fire engine," he recounts, and when he stood up, he felt as if his body was ablaze. Later that evening, John McKaig stood in his living room and prayed, "Lord Jesus Christ, my life is yours. I surrender it all to you."

The transformation was remarkable. "I used to have a four-letter vocabulary. I went to bars and clubs. I was wrapped up in doing things for myself. But from the time I surrendered my life spiritually, emotionally, physically, I was healed.

Mr. McKaig purchased his first Bible a week later. He

laughs that it took him seven days to find one because he had no idea where to look for religious items. "I bought it at G. Fox department store," he says.

Within a year, Mr. McKaig began pursuing ordination to the diaconate. He flunked his first seminary course on aesthetical theology, the study of the Holy Spirit. Mr. McKaig prayed for help, then went on to successfully complete his studies at St. Thomas Seminary in Bloomfield, CT. He was ordained as a permanent deacon in 1977.

A deacon is an ordained Catholic clergyman; once ordained, he remains a deacon for life. Married men may be ordained to the diaconate but may not remarry should they become widowed. Since it is not typically a full-time position, most deacons hold conventional jobs in addition to Church responsibilities.

These Church duties include conducting baptisms, officiating at weddings and funerals, preaching, visiting the sick, serving the needy, and preparing couples for marriage. "We're not mini-priests," Mr. McKaig laughs. "A deacon is a servant of God. We're called to assist the priests with the needy, homeless, shut-ins and imprisoned."

Mr. McKaig has many friends at the parishes he has served. Known as a caring man whose own troubles have made him compassionate, he is deeply loved by those whom he serves. His ministry is summed up by a terminally ill man whom John used to visit: "When John's around, he makes me feel safe."

Since Mr. McKaig also works full-time in his financial planning business, he often is asked how he juggles two jobs. "I don't," is his matter-of-fact reply. "I am a deacon who works. I live my diaconate. You can't go to church on Sunday, take off your church clothes, put on your business coat, and then not be a Christian. My ministry as a deacon is brought into my business. There is no difference between John McKaig, the financial planner, and John McKaig, the deacon."

Whether he is providing financial services, or preaching the Gospel, John McKaig is a servant of God.

Married and Still Dating?

for Chris Rafala

I was picking up my 10-year-old from a birthday party and I was in a hurry.

"Why are you all dressed up?" the hostess asked me, unaccustomed to seeing me in anything except jeans.

"It's date night," I explained, helping my daughter gather her things.

"Date night?" the hostess repeated a little too loudly. Other parents glanced our way.

"Well, yes," I responded. "Saturday night is date night for Peter and me."

I thought that would settle it. Doesn't everyone know what a date is?

"Date night?" the hostess said again with a hint of sarcasm in her voice. "You actually go on dates – with your husband?"

"Yes," I replied, a little annoyed. "Peter and I do a lot for the kids. This is something we do for ourselves."

A nearby parent entered the fray. "Wow. I'm jealous. How did you do it when the kids were little?"

"We hired a babysitter whenever possible," I

explained. "If we couldn't find one, we still designated Saturday night for the two of us. We put the kids to bed early, then ate a quiet meal alone together."

"By candlelight?" a third parent queried.

"Um, yeah, I guess we did eat by candlelight," I replied. "The important thing was that we were relating to one another as adults rather than simply as parents. We think of it as an investment in our marriage."

"Date night," the hostess mused softly. "My husband and I never do that."

Date night. It's a staple of Cram family life and I highly recommend it.

The activities have varied over the years. When we could afford it we've gone out to dinner; other times we've made picnics, enjoyed open-air band concerts, strolled the mall (with a mandatory stop at the cookie shop), or met friends for the evening. We often start our date with the vigil Mass even though we worship as a family Sunday morning. The key element is time together.

The kids know the routine and they don't like it, even after all these years. Several years ago 7-year-old Tierney watched glumly as I prepared to go out. "Whatcha doing?" she asked in her best disapproving voice, knowing full well what I was doing.

"I'm going on a date with Dad," I answered.

"It's stupid to call it a date when you're already married," she pouted.

"I disagree," I replied. "Married dates are awesome because you get to go home together at the end of the evening."

"Cool," she said, brightening a little. "I never

thought of that."

Another time 5-year-old Victoria asked, "Are you goin' someplace?"

"I'm going on a date with my boyfriend," I whispered, flashing Peter a mischievous glance.

Victoria leaned forward with an air of delicious secrecy. "Really? Who?"

The children may not like it but Saturday night dates help keep our marriage vibrant. Too many couples function more like roommates or business partners than lovers, neglecting to nurture their romance.

The consequences of such neglect can be deadly. One of the highest rates of divorce occurs after 20 years of marriage when the nest becomes empty, and spouses find themselves facing a stranger with whom they have little in common.

The irony is that it's not as difficult as people think to keep the romance alive. It's a matter of cherishing one's spouse, thinking about him during the day the way we did during courtship when we could hardly stand to be apart. Sometimes I stuff love notes into my husband's coat pocket, or mail a juicy card to him at the office. He brings home flowers when it's not our anniversary, or calls during the day just to hear my voice.

Recently Peter and I began rereading our old love letters. I joke that the real reason he enjoys my letters is because they gush about how wonderful he is. In truth, the letters rekindle romance and serve as a powerful reminder of the love that drew us together in the first place.

My perspective on romance was reinforced some years ago when I suffered a critical illness. After I was out of danger, Peter called me in the hospital one afternoon, exhausted from tending a houseful of small children and still terribly worried about me. I encouraged him to do something for himself that night to alleviate the stress, rather than visit me.

"Reg," he said, choking up, "I almost lost you. Visiting you *is* doing something for myself."

That evening Peter and I sat on my hospital bed and talked. We held hands, and we shared my lime green Jello-O. It was romance at its finest as we focused on our love for one another and the love of God that glues it together. That date in my hospital room was more romantic than any candlelight dinner will ever be.

Open Letter to Diocesan Priests

for Fr. William Metzler

He sat in our living room, one of your brother priests. It was late and he was exhausted, but still he stayed, soaking up the prayer and encouragement, savoring the laughter and the old Flip Wilson routines and the warmth of friends.

This was not a parish function. It was his day off and he'd come to enjoy homemade pizza, friendly debate, and a recharge for his weary batteries.

His batteries get drained quickly these days but I don't have to tell you that. The priesthood has changed from the era when many of you courageously said 'yes' to God. You no longer occupy a world that values sacrifice, nor are you living in a rectory with three or four priests who buoy your spirits during long days and fractured nights.

Instead, most of you fly solo with a scarcity of backup and a crushing work load. American Catholics confront you with a consumer attitude expecting services, attention and convenience with little understanding of your world.

Sometimes you worry about your health and you wonder what it will take for Catholics to realize that the vocations crisis is not someone else's problem. It's everyone's problem and we'll feel it acutely when Grandma dies and we have to wait a week for the funeral, or when Dad is seriously ill and we have trouble finding a priest to anoint him.

How long will it take for us pew-sitters to make the connection between a pastor who has to drop Masses at linked parishes because he cannot be in two places at once, and our failure to encourage our sons towards the priesthood?

But that's not why I'm writing to you. What I'm wondering is, has anyone thanked you today for being a priest? Has anyone asked to hear the story of your call to the priesthood, then laughed at how mortified you were when the head cheerleader suggested that you'd make a great priest? Has anyone inquired what he can do to lighten your load, or how he can pray for you this week, or if you'd like to use his cottage for a day off? Any chance you've pressed the 'play' button on the answering machine lately and heard, "Hi Father, this is Harry Jackson from the liturgy committee. I'm just calling to remind you that we love you."?

As converts with anti-Catholic attitudes, my husband and I have a unique perspective on priests. When we began to seriously consider the Catholic Church, well-meaning friends issued dire warnings that we'd be committing spiritual suicide. They said we'd never find genuine faith among Catholics and certainly not among priests. You're not going to like this, but priests were depicted as a bunch of power-hungry white guys whose spiritual lives consist of droning empty prayers and planning Bingo games.

Instead, we met you – warm, deeply spiritual men who lead counter-cultural lives and whose faith in action inspires us every day. For heaven's sake, you've given up money, power and sex in order to serve the God of the universe. If that's not radical Christian living, what is?

So I'm writing to say thanks. Thanks for the time you sat with a desolate widow after her husband of 57 years passed away. Thanks for hearing that kid's confession and sending him on his way beaming about how much God loves him, and for the countless nights you lie awake worrying about how to meet the payroll. Thanks for visiting a parishioner's next door neighbor in the hospital, and for skipping your day off the following week in order to conduct the funeral.

Thanks for sacrificing the companionship of a wife in order to serve strangers, including me.

Thanks for giving up the legacy of children so you can devote yourself more fully to living and preaching the Gospel.

God sees it all. He hears you praying the Divine Office in the wee hours with a tattered breviary and a heart that pours itself out to the Father of mercies. He knows your desire to lead a life of holiness, and your yearning for more energy, more laughter, more priests. And He loves you more than you can imagine.

If you ever wonder if you're making a difference in anyone's life, I assure you that you're making a difference in mine. Thank you for pouring out your life for us. You're the greatest.

P.S. Thanks for being a priest.

The Cost of a Life

for Virginia Martin

Remember back to when you were 9 years old. You're playing kickball with your friends when someone asks what you want to be when you grow up. Two boys shout, "Firefighters!"

One kid wants to paint the yellow lines down the middle of the streets and another plans to be the first woman president. The rest are tomorrow's space explorers, truck drivers and priests.

No one wants to be a drug addict.

When I was a kid, my younger sister always had big plans. At age 5 she announced that she wanted to be a tiger when she grew up. Later she aimed for the Olympic diving team, and after that she wanted to be a famous horseback rider.

Eventually she decided to become a nurse or a mother at home.

She didn't become any of these things. Instead, my sister became a drug addict.

It started in junior high with a cigarette snuck from my mother's purse. Before long it was a beer in the woods, then marijuana behind the school gym. By high school she was shooting hard drugs into scarred veins as her grades plummeted and her world descended into a cyclone of deception. The lies led to more lies, and the drugs led to more drugs.

My family was heartbroken. We enlisted every type of help imaginable, and once, my sister was clean and sober for more than a year.

During such times of sobriety, she always returned to her faith, which was rich and deep from years of pain.

But the drugs always lured her back. "The addiction is so strong," she'd admit with shame.

One day long after we were grown, my sister and her newborn baby stopped by for a visit. She'd been sober for a few months but I suspected that she was drifting back into drugs.

"I had some tests while I was pregnant," my sister told me nervously. "Reg, I'm HIV positive."

HIV. That's the virus that causes AIDS, and back in 1986 it was a death sentence.

Without medications and treatments that we have today, babies born to mothers with HIV often contracted the virus as well. I looked at my beautiful nephew with his curly locks and soft mahogany skin, and I wept at the thought that he was as likely to die as he was to live. Such costly mistakes my sister made.

I began to learn about HIV and it made me angry. I was angry that many people with HIV mistakenly thought they weren't contagious if they had no symptoms of illness, so they continued to infect others through drug or sexual contact.

I was angry at those who self-righteously

condemned people with AIDS, as if somehow they were better than everyone else because AIDS had not yet touched that world.

I was frustrated by the ignorance of friends who warned me to keep my children away from the AIDS residence where my sister eventually lived. "What are you afraid of?" I'd ask in exasperation. "You can't catch AIDS by playing 'Go Fish' with someone."

Even within the medical community, bigotry existed. One day I watched a nurse draw blood from a child without using latex gloves. When I inquired about it, the nurse grew indignant.

"This is the suburbs!" she insisted. "Nice little suburban children don't get AIDS!"

Oh, really? That very week I'd spoken with the mother of two nice little suburban children who had AIDS. The virus that causes AIDS is spread through the transfer of blood and body fluids, and it occurs in every community. Yes, even nice little suburban ones.

After living with the virus for seven years, my sister became gravely ill. She had finally freed herself of the drugs and alcohol, and she knew that despite her terrible mistakes, God was cradling her in the crook of His arms.

My sister understood, perhaps better than I ever will, that apart from God's mercy, she had nothing.

And thus she died, a child of God whom He called by name to be His own.

Her name was Marietta.

Clothe the Naked? What Naked?

for Cathy Treacy, who inspires with joy

There's a passage in the Old Testament book of
Isaiah that bugged me. God was rebuking His people
because He didn't like their fasting. Sure, they were
skipping meat on Fridays, or whatever they did back in
ancient Israel, but they were living terrible lives. "This is
the fast that I choose," God had said, "to loose the bonds of
wickedness, to let the oppressed go free . . . to share your
bread with the hungry, and bring the homeless poor into
your house; when you see the naked, to cover them . . ."

I understand feeding the hungry, freeing the
oppressed and providing for the homeless. The part that
always baffled me, however, was that 'covering the naked'
thing. Cover the naked when I see them? I don't know
about you, but there just aren't that many naked people
who wander the streets of my town. How am I supposed to
obey God's command if the problem doesn't present itself?

Never underestimate the power of God.

It happened on a chilly Wednesday morning. I was
running late as I headed out the door to weekday Mass. I
grabbed my husband's fleece jacket and hastily slipped it
over my head, climbed into the car and sped off.

The suburban neighborhoods gradually gave way to more rural roads. I was hurrying down the long, quiet lane to the church when I noticed a police cruiser driving toward me, lights flashing. The police officer was slowly panning house numbers, evidently searching for the origin of a 911 call. Just as the officer passed me and disappeared up what turned out to be the wrong driveway, a frantic woman ran into the road, her face contorted as she shrieked in terror. Her feet and legs were bare, and she was wrapped in a quilt. There was an angry-looking man in the driveway behind her, alternately screaming and begging her to return.

I did not want to leave the scene until the officer reappeared so I pulled over and beckoned the woman into the relative safety of my car.

She quickly climbed in. The woman appeared young and pretty and completely disheveled. She tried to explain what was happening, but she was hysterical and her words did not make sense. It was clear, however, that the man had beaten her and that she was terrified. It sounded as if he had beaten her on previous occasions as well, although it was difficult to understand much of what she was saying.

As she spoke, I realized that she had wrapped herself in a bedspread because she was not yet dressed. In other words, she was naked.

I peeled off Peter's fleece jacket and helped the woman pull it over her head. She was freezing. And I wondered, what kind of fear would induce a woman to run out into the road wearing only a bedspread?

I drove toward the driveway where the officer had disappeared, intercepting him as he reemerged. With kindness, he helped the young woman into the cruiser. Two additional police cars arrived to deal with the angry-looking man, who was still begging the woman to return. I gave what little information I could, wished the woman well, and continued on my way to Mass, shaken.

About a week later, I saw a moving truck emptying the contents of the small house. I never learned what happened. I hope the woman is safe.

When I returned home after Mass that day, I explained to my husband that I'd given away his favorite fleece jacket. Only then did I realize what God had done. He had demonstrated that even here, in a sleepy New England town, people can be hungry and naked and oppressed. And if we wish to please God, we must care for them with generosity and love, as God, in His tenderness, cares for us.

A Final Good-Bye

for Fr. Kevin Forsyth, and Aubrey

It was a wake and funeral all in one, and I couldn't stop laughing. Six-year-old Victoria solemnly led the funeral procession through the living room, carrying the powder blue 'Jesus Loves Me' cross high above her tiny frame. She was closely followed by 9-year-old Tierney, clad in hand-me-down pajamas and bearing the miniature casket. It was actually an old jewelry box that once housed gaudy earrings but had become the final resting place for Tierney's beloved goldfish, Goldie. The casket was decked out with festive pebbles for the occasion and the dead fish had been gently laid to rest across the top.

Last in the procession was 12-year-old Meredith, carrying the Bible and her carefully prepared notes for the funeral service which she had planned with gentleness to help soothe her sister's grief. Thirteen-year-old Skip sprawled out on the living room sofa wearing his coolest sunglasses (to hide his weeping eyes, he announced with a smirk).

I held myself together during the off-key rendition of 'Amazing Grace' but began to lose my grip as Meredith greeted the mourners with a somber voice.

"Good evening," she intoned. "Tonight we are gathered to remember the fish, Gold Cram." ("*Sniff, sniff*" I thought I heard from Skip's corner until a quick glance revealed his impish grin.)

"Please join in prayer," Meredith continued. "Eternal rest grant unto him, O Lord, and let perpetual light shine upon him." "Amen," we all chimed. I bit the inside of my cheek to keep from giggling.

After another hymn, Tierney approached the pulpit for the first Scripture reading. I don't remember having seen a lector in pajamas before but perhaps I just haven't paid attention. Tierney read the passage about how we need fear no calamity because we have placed our trust in the One who is eternal. The problem was that when she got to the word 'calamity,' she pronounced it more like 'calamari.'

My husband and I erupted in gales of laughter. "We're burying a fish, and you're talking about calamari!" Peter choked. Meredith shot him a dirty look and Victoria took it all in, quietly noting appropriate funeral etiquette.

After a few kind words about the brief life of Goldie the goldfish, the service ended with a closing hymn that was not a hymn at all, but rather a poem about a beetle named Alexander who lived in a match box until his nanny set him loose by mistake. The appropriateness was shaky at best, but seeing as this was a funeral for a fish, we let it slide.

As the service concluded, the casket was gently carried out of the living room, then unceremoniously dumped onto the kitchen counter, where it sat for two days.

By that point Tierney's tears had long since dried, as

had the fish. When the third day dawned, rich with religious symbolism, I insisted that either Tierney bury her long-deceased friend, or else Gold Cram would become a permanent part of our compost heap.

Thus Goldie the goldfish found his final resting place amidst the pines in our front yard, marked by a simple pebble cross and two banana peels.

Our funeral provided valuable instruction to young Victoria, who has committed to memory important guidelines for grief: Dark glass and feet pajamas are appropriate attire for wakes; raucous laughter is welcome; and remember to close the casket before you go outside to play.

"Let the children come to Me and do not hinder them, for to such as these belongs the kingdom of God." Jesus

Custody of the Eyes

for Ron and Carol Legler

I was scurrying around the recycling center sorting glass, newspapers, and corrugated cardboard. Somewhere between the plastics and the scrap metal I noticed a man looking at me. He wasn't exactly staring but he was gazing more intently than I cared for. He sauntered in my direction and smiled at me. I nodded vaguely and continued sorting plastics.

A moment later he passed me again. "Hi," he said with a friendly smile. "Um, hi," I responded, and kept moving. I began hauling trash cans to the dumpster when he strolled over and offered, "Need any help?"

"No thanks," I stated, escaping towards a group of retirees discussing the day's news.

A moment later he was back again. "I'm Mike Harris," he said with that same smile.

"Oh," I stammered. "Hi." I was growing uneasy so I finished my task in record time. He was still watching me.

I quickly climbed into my car but Mr. Persistent was right behind me. "Nice to meet you!" he called out as I closed the door. "Want to have lunch some time?"

I drove away.

At dinner that evening we had a lively family discussion about the incident, especially after I commented that I'm not used to guys trying to hit up on me.

"That's 'hit on me,' Mom," one teenager corrected with a groan.

"Yeah, well, it's been a while," I said, glancing at my husband of 22 years who found the incident sort of amusing. I mean, who gets picked up at the dump? There's something singularly unromantic about hauling smelly trash cans from a minivan that's decorated with crushed Cheerios and french fries.

"What did the guy look like, Mom?" a curious teenager inquired.

"I don't know," I shrugged.

"What do you mean you don't know?" she pressed. "You looked at him, didn't you?"

"Well, no, actually I didn't" I replied. "He was trying to pick me up. Why would I want to look at him?"

A younger child piped up. "But Mom, it doesn't hurt to just look. Remember what Auntie Etta used to say? 'Just because you're on a diet doesn't mean you can't look at the menu.'"

"I remember, sweetheart, but I don't agree. Sometimes it can hurt to just look. Do you remember the story of Abraham and Lot?"

"Abraham who?" she asked. "You mean Abraham Lincoln?"

The older kids giggled.

"No, sweetheart, Abraham in the Bible, and his nephew Lot," I explained.

"What does that have to do with the guy at the dump?

"Everything," I replied. "Abraham and Lot's families shared the same land until their herds became too big. Lot liked the appearance of the lush Jordan valley where the wicked cities of Sodom and Gomorrah were located, so he headed in that direction while Abraham headed in the opposite direction. By the end of the story, Lot's wife was dead, his daughters had been offered as prostitutes, and Lot barely escaped with his life."

"I still don't understand,' the teens complained. "What does that have to do with Mr. Romance at the dump?"

"Lot's problems began when he glanced toward Sodom," I continued. "He liked what he saw so he headed to the valley and pitched his tent outside the city. In the next chapter he was living inside the city gates, and before you know it he was a leader in Sodom, ensnared by evil and offering his own daughters as prostitutes. Lot was a righteous man but he got into trouble when he didn't run away from temptation. Instead he gradually edged closer to the darkness, almost as if he was flirting with it. He hadn't counted on the temptation winning."

"Yeah, and his wife got into trouble when she looked back at the burning city of Sodom after God said not to, and God zapped her into a pillar of salt!" a kid oozed with enthusiasm.

"But back to that guy," a teen pressed with an unsettled voice, "You wouldn't have really been tempted by him, would you, Mom?"

"No, actually, I wouldn't have," I answered honestly.

"But even good people succumb to temptation when their eyes linger too long. That's why it's wise to run away, even if you're only being tempted to take a quick look. Being faithful with our eyes leads to being faithful with our lives – and faithfulness is cool. Way cooler than any guy at the dump."

Immaculee

Note: This story contains descriptions of violence

Immaculee Ilibagiza enjoyed an idyllic childhood in a close-knit Catholic family. Her parents were hard-working teachers whose kindnesses touched nearly everyone in the village. Immaculee had a promising future as an educated young Rwandan woman, studying electronic and mechanical engineering at the university.

But civil unrest was brewing between the Hutu and Tutsi tribes in Rwanda. When Hutus seized power in 1994, they instituted a campaign of Tutsi annihilation. Hutu death squads slaughtered one million Tutsis and Tutsi sympathizers in a span of just 100 days. Neighbor murdered neighbor, often by hand or with machete. No one was spared.

As the genocide began, Immaculee's father sent her to the home of a local Hutu pastor, who hid Immaculee in a tiny bathroom along with five other terrified Tutsi women. The pastor bluntly warned the fugitives, "If you make any noise, you will die."

The bathroom was 3 feet by 4 feet – so tiny that they could neither sit nor stand, but had to crouch almost on top of one another. Outside the high window, the women could hear the blood-curdling screams of their countrymen being hacked to death by lifelong friends, as the genocide reached a fevered pitch.

Immaculee expected that the violence would quickly subside, allowing her to return to her beloved family within a few days. But days became weeks. Two additional Tutsi women arrived, bringing the number to eight in the tiny bathroom. Day and night, they crouched in total silence, terrified that the slightest movement would alert the Hutu death squads to their presence. Angry Hutu killers routinely ransacked the house, screaming Immaculee's name and vowing to rape and dismember her when they found her.

The only possession Immaculee carried into hiding was her father's rosary beads. During the early days, she clung to the rosary for solace as she begged God to save her parents and three brothers. As time dragged on, however, negativity overtook her. Anger and resentment about her situation ate away at her faith. She began to pray the rosary as a way of drowning out the negativity inside her. Gradually, she began to feel peace. Immaculee resolved to pray every waking moment in captivity, and yet she could not bring herself to pray for the killers. Finally, after weeks of sleeplessness, she relented and began to pray for her enemies. Only then was she able to sleep soundly.

In addition to praying constantly, Immaculee taught herself English using only two books and a French/English dictionary, translating one word at a time. She hoped to work for the United Nations if she survived the genocide, and English was required. She knew she'd also need proof

84

that she was formally educated, but her documents were hundreds of miles away at a university that lay in ruins.

After 91 days in the bathroom, Immaculee escaped to a French refugee camp. She weighed 65 pounds. All along the roads, bodies were stacked as high as buildings. Land mines were everywhere. Villages were decimated. Commerce had come to a halt. Shortly after her escape, Immaculee heard the crushing news that her entire family had been slaughtered, with the sole exception of a brother who was studying 1,000 miles away in Senegal.

Immaculee was able to secure a ride to her university. Her dorm room had been ransacked and badly damaged, but miraculously, she found $30 of her scholarship money. Even more wonderfully, she unearthed her high school diploma and university progress report that were buried in the rubble. With proof of education, Immaculee was eventually hired by the U.N. to do clerical work, and later, to track relief supplies coming into Rwanda from around the world.

Immaculee's final step was to visit the local prison to confront the man who had butchered her mother and her beloved brother, Damascene. Before the genocide, the killer had been a successful Hutu businessman whose children had been Immaculee's playmates. She remembered him as tall and handsome, with expensive suits. What she saw at the prison appalled her. He was a filthy, emaciated shell of a man. His skin was sallow and bruised; his feet were covered with open sores.

Immaculee was overcome with compassion for this man whose life had been destroyed by sin.

The killer never said a word. He slumped on the

floor sobbing as the warden screamed and insulted him, expecting Immaculee to do the same.

When Immaculee finally spoke, she said simply, "I forgive you."

With God's help, it is possible to forgive the unforgivable.

The Gift

for Mirja Johanson

It was the week before Christmas and I was exhausted.

Our four kids were split among three different schools, I was immersed in a difficult family situation, and for three long years my husband had been working crazy hours in preparation for Y2K. This particular week I had driven more than 600 miles in a minivan that was in worse shape than I was. The front windows wouldn't close more than halfway. The sliding door was wired shut so it wouldn't fall off again. The radio was dead, leaving the clock permanently 49 minutes behind. Well, except during daylight savings time, when it was an hour and 49 minutes behind.

That fall Peter had begun working 90-hour weeks as Y2K closed in. By Thanksgiving he was on call around the clock and came home only to sleep and change clothes. Weekends no longer existed. Forget holidays.

By the week before Christmas Y2K was only 15 days away. Peter was able to function on adrenaline but I had reached a state of physical and emotional exhaustion. And it was my birthday.

In the midst of the craziness Peter and I managed to slip away for a quiet birthday dinner. That's when he astounded me with the most remarkable birthday gift I have ever received. He sent me away alone. Immediately.

I mean really alone, to a tiny mountain village tucked in the crook of the Housatonic River. The Appalachian Trail wound through the nearby state forest, and the only neighbors lived peacefully in the cemetery next door. It was dark, deserted and lonely, and I loved every minute of it.

For three whole days I didn't have to referee a single sibling argument. I could eat Wheaties for dinner if I felt like it, and drink my morning coffee without needing to reheat it even once. There was no telephone, no traffic, no schedule. It was glorious.

I took leisurely walks along the river and listened to the quiet gurgle of water slurping over the stones. I had the unspeakable joy of attending Mass each morning, then lingering in front of the Blessed Sacrament to savor the mystical gift of Christ's presence in the Eucharist. I spent untold hours pouring out my heart to God and listening to the still, small voice of His Holy Spirit. I was like a child climbing onto my daddy's lap and nestling against the soft beating of His Sacred Heart, simply enjoying the pleasure of His company.

Somehow Peter made it through Y2K despite the precious hours dedicated to carpools instead of computer code, and gradually the noisy cadence of our lives returned to a dull roar. But I will always cherish my husband's extraordinary gift, lavished on me to nurture my soul, and because he loves me.

We joke that for my birthday, my husband got rid of me. But the truth is that Peter's gift was enormously sacrificial, modeled after the One who sent an even greater gift to a weary and discouraged world. That gift was the most glorious, most tender, most sacrificial gift the world has ever known – Christmas.

To Dance With the Prodigal

for Tierney, whose passion for God inspires me

"Why should I forgive her? What has she ever done except disrupt this family and cause us pain?"

The teenager hurled the words into the stony silence of her empty bedroom. She was furious with her younger sister for disrupting the family again. This time, her sister had stolen money for drugs, then she'd run away. Her parents had been frantic for weeks, but now that she was back, everyone was fawning over her like she was some conquering hero returning from battle.

"I've been here all along and they certainly don't fawn over me," the older sister thought to herself as she skulked up the stairs. "They barely notice me."

She tried to say this to her parents, but her mother just told her to read the story of the Prodigal Son.

She hated that story. It always seemed that the older brother got a bad deal. In the story, the younger brother had greedily demanded his inheritance while the father was still alive, then he'd squandered it on foolishness. Starving and desperate, the son returned home in shame to beg the father's forgiveness. Instead of punishing him, however, the father threw a big party. To make it worse, when the older brother complained that he didn't get enough attention, nobody seemed to care. No one even seemed to notice.

That's why she hated the story. It reminded her of her own life.

I wish I could say that the older sister found peace as the years went on, but she didn't. It wasn't until she was an adult and had a prodigal of her own that she finally grasped it. I know this for sure, because I am that older sister.

The funny thing is that my special prodigal is not even a real person. She's a tattered stuffed bunny named Susannah.

Susannah began life in the crib of our infant daughter, Tierney. At the beginning, Susannah was clean and soft and well-behaved, sitting quietly as Tierney's chubby fists squashed her velvety fur. But like many of us, Susannah gradually became gray and balding, and the stuffing bunched around the middle.

How Tierney loved her.

For the next eight years, Tierney and Susannah were inseparable. Susannah was so well known around town that people greeted her by name as if she was as real as the child who carried her. When I used a baby carrier to cradle our newborn against my chest, Tierney tied a bandana around her belly so she could carry Susannah. During outings to the beach, Susannah sat on the towel to guard Tierney's pail and shovel from crabs and fishies. It was a sweet and powerful love.

Unfortunately, Susannah developed the bad habit of wandering off when Tierney wasn't looking. Once it was at the grocery store. Another time, Susannah ran away at the shopping center, and then it was the sandbox at school. We always managed to find her until that terrible day when Tierney was 8. That's when Susannah got lost for real.

We searched every closet and every cubby. We scoured the garage and turned the house upside down, but we could not find her. Poor Tierney was heartbroken. Susannah was on Tierney's mind every night as she fell asleep with empty arms, and every morning as she drowsily reached for her tattered friend before remembering that Susannah wasn't there. For months on end, Tierney never stopped looking and she never stopped grieving.

Then came the scream of delight when Susannah was discovered in an unused trash bin. Tierney was almost incoherent with joy as she clutched her beloved bunny and sobbed. Oblivious to the world, they danced around like lovers, spinning and laughing and kissing and weeping.

And as I watched, I could picture the father running to meet his wayward son, sobbing with joy.

It humbled me, and reminded me again why Jesus came among us. Yes, it was for dutiful older siblings, but also for wandering prodigals who sometimes lose their way.

And until they come home, God never stops looking and He never stops grieving. And He never gives up.

Lessons From the Wee Hours

for Don and Elise Strickland, the best neighbors ever

I'll spare you the boring details; suffice it to say that I've developed an auto-immune form of arthritis that strikes people in their 30's and 40's. For months the pain kept me awake at night, rendering me completely exhausted. I walked with a cane and my body was covered with psoriasis lesions. I felt like a leper.

Fortunately a newly developed injectable drug has eased the symptoms. Along the way, I've done a lot of thinking, especially during those long, sleepless nights. Here are some things I've learned:

- Nobody heard of Psoriatic Arthritis until Phil Mickelson began doing commercials for a prescription drug.
- Canes are available in ergonomically correct models, designed for either right hand or left hand.
- The newspaper is delivered at 4:30 a.m.
- Everybody is in pain, or used to be in pain, plans to be in pain, or knows somebody in pain, and hence knows all about my experience.
- People are enthusiastic about praying for their friends, even if they don't normally pray. I have a

funny feeling that God enjoys hearing from these people most of all.

- Doughnuts make everything a little bit better.
- When you're in pain in the middle of the night, everyone else is asleep.
- Kids are incredibly understanding. Then four seconds later, they forget.
- Hold the cane on your good side.
- A sink full of dirty dishes is not nearly as important as telling a bedtime story to your kid or grandkid.
- Rheumatology overlaps with neurology and orthopedics. The patient has to figure out which is needed.
- If you're under 35 and you use a cane, people assume you had a sports injury. If you're between 35 and 50, they assume an accident. Between 50 and 75, knee replacement surgery. After that, they pay no attention.
- MRI's and bone scans cost what I paid in annual college tuition.
- People in poor nations live in more pain than those in wealthy nations.
- Being weak makes us truly depend on God.
- You haven't lived till you've handed a loaded hypodermic needle to the teenager administering your shot, as the kid asks, "Are you *sure* I have to clean my room, Mom?"
- Bible stories about people with leprosy are suddenly alive with meaning.
- Beginning an expensive new drug requires more approvals than getting hired as a newspaper

columnist.

- Google is awesome.
- It's amazing how natural it is to talk with God when you're alone in the middle of the night.
- Small children instinctively pick up a dropped cane and hand it back to the owner.
- When someone brings you Communion at home, it creates a forever bond.
- Nobody talks in doctors' waiting rooms.
- Everybody talks in medical lab waiting rooms.
- When you fall asleep while sitting on a stool, you wake up just in time to feel the crash.
- High heels are incompatible with a cane. I learned this the hard way.
- When caring people want to be helpful, they give advice.
- The guy who decided to put the rheumatology office on the far corner of the 10th floor never had arthritis.
- Medical insurance is not a luxury.
- Nine out of 10 Americans believe that dark chocolate has magic power.
- If you ask God to teach you humility, be prepared to duck.

What Is It Like to Die?

for Mary Smith, with great love

Five-year-old Meggie had been battling leukemia for more than half of her young life. The disease went into remission for a while, but when it returned, it was stronger than ever and no treatment could slow its growth. By the time Meggie entered kindergarten, it was clear to everyone that she was going to lose the battle.

Her parents tried to prepare themselves for Meggie's death, but how can one prepare for the unthinkable? Meggie was such a spitfire. She had remained cheerful even when radiation sapped her strength and chemotherapy snatched away her dark curls. She was a favorite at the children's hospital, serenading fussy babies with her off-key voice until they grinned at her with their bald heads and toothless smiles.

From her earliest days, Meggie had bubbled over with curiosity and enthusiasm, sometimes exasperating her parents by asking questions from morning until long after dark. Where do fireflies sleep? Why do we have toes? When Mary and Joseph went on a date, who baby-sat for baby Jesus? Do giants have belly buttons? Why doesn't Big Bird live with a grown-up?

As Meggie grew sicker, her questions focused increasingly on death, and yet she did not speak in the frightened hush tones typically used by adults. Instead, she was as matter-of-fact about death as she was about frogs and belly buttons and ice cream cones. What would happen to her body after she died? Would Santa Claus know where to find her? Would her parents give her toys to another little girl? Could she take her teddy bear with her to heaven? Does Jesus have a teddy bear?

Meggie's parents were able to answer most of the child's questions, but they dreaded the day when Meggie asked about the actual process of dying. The truth was, they had no idea. How could they explain something they didn't understand themselves?

Sure enough, the day finally arrived. "Mama, what is it like to die?" Meggie asked with innocent curiosity. "Will it hurt? Will I be scared? Will you be with me?" Meggie's innocence pierced her mother's heart, and yet at that precise moment, she knew exactly what to say.

"You know how sometimes you get scared in the middle of the night?" her mother began. "When that happens, you run across the hall to our room and climb into bed with Daddy and me, right?"

Meggie nodded her head, her dark eyes capturing every word.

"When you wake up the next morning, where are you, sweetheart?" her mother continued.

Meggie had never thought of that before. "I'm back in my own bed," she answered in surprise.

"That's right," her mother explained. "While you're asleep, your Daddy picks you up in his big, strong arms and carries you back to your bed where you belong.

"That's what it's like to die. We're here on earth for only a little while, sweetheart. Then, when the time is right, our heavenly Father picks us up in His big, strong arms and gently carries us home to heaven, which is where we really belong anyway."

"Oh," said Meggie with a contented sigh. "That's not scary at all."

And so it was that a few weeks later Meggie quietly slipped into a coma. The following night, her heavenly Father picked her up in His big, strong arms and gently carried her home to where she really belonged.

Yearnings of the Heart

for Dickie, Pat and Carla, who walk with me through the valleys

Peter and I had been married for three years. We were young and healthy, and finally ready to start a family.

We had it all planned out. I'd get pregnant with our first child, resign from my position with IBM, and become a mom at home. We'd have three children in rapid succession so they'd be close in age. Maybe we'd go wild by having a fourth child. Peter's job was secure and we were thrifty, so the plan seemed solid.

But months passed without a pregnancy, then a year. Two years. Doctors poked me with needles. I submitted to drugs, hormones and painful tests. Still no pregnancy.

The yearning for a child was profound, rising from deep within my being. Why would God instill in me such a yearning, then deny its fulfillment? It made no sense.

One day I read a Bible story in the book of II Samuel about young King David. He had disobeyed God, so God instructed him to build an altar on the threshing floor of a certain Jebusite man, in order to make a sacrifice to the Lord. King David approached the man and asked to purchase the threshing floor, but the Jebusite man offered it free of charge, along with oxen and wood.

King David declined the generous offer, insisting instead on paying full price. "I will not offer to God a sacrifice that costs me nothing," the king explained.

I read that again: "I will not offer to God a sacrifice that costs me nothing."

What did that mean?

I thought about Lent. If I hate brussels sprouts, it's not much of a sacrifice to give up brussels sprouts for Lent. Instead, I might give up chocolate, or television, or Facebook. Why? Because I want to offer to God a sacrifice that costs me something.

Did this mean I had to sacrifice to God my plan for children? In fact, wasn't I supposed to submit to God every plan for my life, in favor of His plan?

To be honest, the thought terrified me. I mean, I had dreams for my life. What if God disappointed me?

God had never disappointed me before, so gradually, painfully, I began to relinquish my vise-grip on my life. "Not my will, but Your will," I prayed often, even when I wasn't sure I meant it. "Not my will, but Your will."

And still I was not pregnant.

But it did happen. As we began our seventh year of marriage, we welcomed a son, Peter, Jr., a.k.a. Skip. A year and a half later, our joy was magnified with the arrival of a daughter, Meredith, followed by another daughter, Tierney. And yes, we were outlandish enough to have a fourth child, Victoria, We were ecstatic. Truth be told, we couldn't wait to have a fifth and a sixth child. But I get ahead of myself.

It was a scorching July day when I gave birth to Victoria. The baby was perfect but I suffered a complication during labor. The next thing I knew, I was groggily regaining consciousness in the Intensive Care Unit. I could hear nurses talking quietly. "Who's going to tell her?" one nurse whispered. "Not me!" said another. "It's going to break her heart. You tell her."

The news did break my heart. The complication had been catastrophic, and lifesaving measures had included extreme emergency surgery. What she was trying to say was that I was no longer able to bear children.

I cried for 10 years.

Friends were baffled by my reaction. I mean, we had four children; how much could a girl want?

But family size was supposed to be *my* decision. It was *my* choice. Why should that choice be snatched away by some random act of nature?

Once again, I struggled to sacrifice my plans to God's tender care. Once again, it was a sacrifice that cost me dearly. It was no easier the second time around.

Relinquishing our plans to God is hard. For me, the struggle revolved around family; others wrestle with health, career, or marriage. The fundamental question is the same: will I, or will I not submit my carefully arranged plans to God? Can I trust Him? And if I do, will God meet my deepest needs?

God answered this question long ago through the prophet Jeremiah. "I know the plans I have for you, says the Lord, plans for good and not for evil, to give you a future and a hope."

That's good enough for me.

God Works Together for Good

for Peter, who makes my dreams come true

I hate minivans. It didn't start that way. I used to love the storage space and the extra bench that allowed me to separate warring factions when a kid whined, "She looked at me!" But after 15 years of cruising the suburban lanes with millions of other boxes on wheels, I'm tired of minivans. They may be practical but they are dull as dust.

Truth be told, what I really want is a Volkswagen Beetle. Convertible, In robin's egg blue. Is that too much to ask?

About 10 years ago, a neighboring family had four active teenagers and a minivan. One day the mother reached the end of her minivan rope so she drove to the local car dealership, traded in the minivan, and returned to the neighborhood in a red two-seater sports car.

At the time I thought she was crazy. How was she going to get her kids to swim practice? Where would she fit the hockey sticks and groceries? How could they drive to church together?

The woman didn't care. She simply informed her family that if they wanted to get somewhere, they could arrange their own rides because she couldn't possible fit them into her cute little sports car.

She lasted about three months. Sure enough, one day the cute little sports car disappeared and a boring minivan appeared in its place.

Now that I have almost four teenagers, I understand my neighbor's desperation. Many days I've been tempted to drive my industrial gray van to the local Volkswagen dealer for a trade, but I'm sure he'd laugh me off the lot. Why would he want a minivan when he can drive a Volkswagen?

Besides, my husband needs a lot of storage space. The last time Peter threw anything away was around 1975 when he reluctantly parted with his childhood penny candy receipts. The guy has been know to pack half his worldly possessions just to visit the dentist.

So why am I writing this? One sunny day, I was minding my own business at a stop light when a guy going 40 m.p.h. crashed into the back of my adorable, industrial gray minivan. He never saw me. The next thing I knew, my van was thrust forward with a loud scraping noise, shoving me nearly 30 feet ahead.

The other guy's airbag deployed and the back of my van crumpled like an accordion. Both cars were totaled. Remarkably, no one was hurt. As the police diagrammed the crash scene a short while later, I sat in the front of my demolished van wondering how we'd manage with just my husband's compact car. That's when a dastardly thought occurred to me: Maybe I could get a Volkswagen Beetle out of the deal. Convertible. In robin's egg blue.

When I broached the subject with Peter that evening, he looked at me as if I'd been sniffing too much laundry detergent. A Beetle? One of those little bug things? How could we fit his golf clubs and triathlon gear into a trunk

103

the size of a mailbox?

I self-righteously informed him that the new Beetles are much better than the old ones, thank you very much. They even have heat. But I acknowledged that it probably couldn't hold his lifetime supply of broken computer monitors so, dejected, I consented to the purchase of a dull, used station wagon with a dump sticker. Did I mention that it was dull?

Christmas rolled around a few weeks later. At the end of a delightful morning, Peter assembled the kids, aimed a camera at my face, and handed me a small package. The card said something about how we were approaching our 25th wedding anniversary and that he'd marry me all over again.

Inside the wrapping was a jewelry box. To be honest, I groaned silently. I'm not a big jewelry lover and yet it was obvious that Peter was giving me something quite special. I planted my best plastic smile on my face and planned to ooh and aah appropriately.

I opened the jewelry box and my jaw dropped. Nestled inside was a Volkswagen key chain. In my speechless moment, Peter explained that the minivan accident made it possible for us to add a VW to the family. Beetle. Convertible.

It arrived two months later in a blizzard but we didn't care. We drove home with the top down as we praised God for turning our sorrow into joy.

Did I mention that it's robin's egg blue?

"In all things God works together for good to those who love Him and are called according to His purpose." Rom. 8:28

Mental Illness Poster Child

for Father Jerome Machar, O.C.S.O

"Please, Lord, this is not what I want to be known for! Can't you understand that?"

The thoughts spilled out through my tears. I've been blessed with such riches: a great marriage, four incredible kids, a lifetime of work with teenagers, opportunities to write and speak. I wouldn't mind being remembered for any of these.

I don't want to be remembered for my long battle with mental illness. It's been painful enough to live through it; I have no desire to live it a second time through my writing. Was it too much to ask that God give me privacy in the matter?

My struggle with mental illness may have started as far back as my teenage years; it's hard to know where normal teenage angst ends and mental illness begins.

I do know that in my twenties and thirties, occasional bouts of depression would descend, lasting several months or longer. Then, for no apparent reason, the darkness would lift and I'd be fine, sometimes for years.

There were other times when I was so irritable that I wanted to crawl out of my skin. My mind would race for days. I was agitated and fidgety and unable to sleep. One episode occurred while Peter and I were alone together for a romantic getaway. During our final dinner, overlooking a spectacular sunset, I became so testy and argumentative that he finally walked out. "Who are you and what have you done with my wife?" he asked sharply.

I had no idea. We assumed that my moods were entirely within my control and that if I just gritted my teeth and exercised some discipline, I could overcome whatever this was. In other words, it was my fault.

Years passed, often quite normal. The time came, however, when an episode began and never went away. Weeks stretched into months, then years. Counseling did not help. I finally visited my doctor, who prescribed a variety of antidepressants. They didn't help, either.

It was during the week of 9/11 while America was focused on the terrorist attacks, that I was absorbed in a crisis of my own. By that point I had grown so depressed and confused that I was no longer able to function in everyday life. That's when my husband stepped in and arranged for me to see a specialist in psychiatric medicine.

The doctor recognized my symptoms as BiPolar Disorder, a mental illness characterized by uncontrollable mood swings due to a chemical imbalance in the brain. It took a long time to find an effective treatment but it did happen. Ever so slowly, order was restored to my life. Music returned, and laughter, and joy.

It took longer to make my peace with the diagnosis. At first I was ashamed. I could hardly spit out the words, 'mental illness.' That was for other people – troubled people – but certainly not for me.

My attitude gradually shifted as friends and family

surrounded me with love. My father called from Virginia every week for a year. My mother provided a sympathetic shoulder since she, too, had struggled with mental illness. An old friend delivered dinner to us every Tuesday night for more than six months. My pastor checked in often to be sure I was getting the medical help I needed. Not a single person chastised me, blamed me, or told me to pick myself up by my bootstraps. Instead, they encouraged me to treat mental illness with the same compassion that I apply to physical illness. Slowly, imperceptibly, I began to heal.

One day I asked my middle school kid if she was embarrassed that her mother suffers from mental illness. She didn't understand the question. "What are you talking about, Mom? If you're sick, you're sick. There's nothing to be embarrassed about."

What a delightful attitude. If only it had come so easily to me. But eventually it did come, and if you saw me now, you would never guess the dark alleys I traveled before making my way into daylight.

Nevertheless I do not like writing about it. I'm tired of talking about it, tired of thinking about it, tired of living it. I don't want to be the Mental Illness Poster Child. I just want to be normal, like everyone else.

But this is who I am, so when the Holy Spirit urges me to write, I write, even when I do not wish to do so. Mental illness may not be the legacy I choose, but perhaps my struggle can be a solace to another, giving hope where there are only shadows and despair.

May God bless the poor in spirit, for theirs is the kingdom of God.

The Church's Quiet Heroes

for Betty Weaver

As Mass ended, my friend and I followed the crowd into the warm sunshine. We greeted the priest, then proceeded to the shade of a nearby tree to chat.

"You know what bugs me?" my friend Annie complained, seemingly out of nowhere. "Why do all of our clergy have to be celibate? How can they possibly understand married life, or children, or the workplace, when all they know is celibacy? It was clear that she had been stewing about this matter for a while.

"But not all clergy are celibate," I began.

"Yes, they are!" Annie interrupted. "Priests cannot be married. Everyone knows that."

"But priests are not the only clergy in the Catholic Church. What about deacons?"

Annie was silent for a moment. "Um, what about deacons?" she asked tentatively.

"Deacons are ordained clergymen of the Catholic Church," I explained. "They can be married, and have children and grandchildren. Most hold regular jobs. A typical deacon lives in a neighborhood and mows the lawn and coaches his kid's soccer team."

"And they're clergy?" Annie asked, incredulous. "I mean, real clergy?"

"They sure are," I assured my friend. "Deacons go through seminary and are ordained for life by the bishop. They preach at Masses. They baptize babies, prepare couples for marriage, conduct wakes and certain wedding ceremonies, and they assist the priests in caring for God's people. Personally, I think deacons are the Church's quiet heroes."

Annie was still unsure. "You know the guy up front who wears the sash across his robe? Is he the deacon?"

"That's him," I replied. "The sash is the deacon's stole, which symbolizes his vocation. During Mass, the deacon typically proclaims the Gospel and sometimes he preaches. He also assists the priest in the liturgy of the Eucharist.

"Is our deacon married?" Annie inquired, gaining interest.

"Yes. His wife usually sits about halfway down the center aisle, on the left. You'd recognize her."

Annie looked like she was having trouble absorbing all this new information, so I decided to tell her about some deacons I know.

"Our parish deacon works with Peter and me, and other married couples, in the Engaged Couples ministry. Engaged couples from around the diocese attend a seminar at which a team of presenters helps prepare the couples for Christian marriage. Typically, a team comprises two lay couples and a deacon and his wife. Our deacon is a fantastic bridge between the engaged couples and the Church because he is a member of the clergy as well as a

109

married man. I love it when he and his wife are on the team.

Annie was listening intently.

I continued. "My family are all converts, and it was a deacon who first helped usher us into the Catholic Church years ago. He came to our house to meet us and answer our endless questions. He wore regular clothes, worked in a regular job, and talked about his wife and kids. In fact, he, too, is a convert, so he understood what we were going through. He was the perfect person to welcome us to the Catholic Church. Now, years later, he is preparing our daughter and her fiance for marriage.

"I've seen deacons bring Communion to strangers, console the bereaved, laugh with teenagers, and load the moving van for a mission trip. Once I watched a deacon kneel in front of the tabernacle to pray with a child who was having nightmares. Our deacons are gems."

"Wow. I had no idea," Annie admitted.

As I headed home, it occurred to me that as Catholics, we have the best of both worlds: priests who are free to serve without the limitations of a wife and children, and deacons who have the richness of family life.

God's design is always perfect.

The Secret Life of Ducks

for Odin Maciolek

There's no easy way to say this so I'll just spit it out. I sleep with a stuffed yellow duck named Goober. Yes, I'm serious.

Goober is adorable in a homely sort of way, with beady eyes and a sprig of hair on the crown of his pointy head that makes him look dorky but sweet. No matter what anyone says, I think Goober is awesome. Even if he isn't the brightest crayon in the box.

Goober's life began in the Easter basket of my teenage daughter Meredith many years back. His existence was so miserable, however, that one day Goober snuck across the hall to my room and never went back. Personally I think he's much happier with me. Don't get Meredith started on that topic.

Not long after Goober came to live with me, I tried to give the guy a proper name. You know, something classy like Melvin or Nigel or McAllister. But no. That girl overheard my plan and she threatened me.

My own kid threatened me! She said she'd take Goober back if I changed his name. I don't think that's legal because it would be like undoing an adoption, and besides,

111

Goober would be devastated, but Meredith wouldn't budge. That girl gets her stubbornness from her father.

To answer your question, no, my husband is not thrilled about sharing his wife with a stuffed duck, no matter how adorable he is (the duck, not the husband). Personally, I think I'm a bargain. I don't chase other men, I'm home at night, and I make great hot fudge sauce. I even laugh at his jokes. What's not to like? I just happen to have a thing for a homely stuffed duck.

By now you're probably wondering about my sanity, not to mention what this has to do with living our faith in everyday life. Well, I have an important point to make if you'll stop interrupting me: Goober teaches me about God's faithfulness. It may sound crazy but it happens to be true. Let me explain.

Last summer I chaperoned a group of a teens to a Steubenville Youth Conference. (I know, it's scary to think that I'm the most mature adult they could find.) Franciscan University of Steubenville sponsors high school youth conferences around the country for teens, and the weekends are superb.

Throughout the weekend I carried with me a small backpack with life's essentials: Bible, water bottle, chocolate chip cookies, and Goober.

Yes, I'm serious. (Why do you keep asking if I'm serious?) We hadn't been at the conference for more than 10 minutes when Goober was snatched from my loving arms and passed around like a beach ball at a rock concert. It was Goober's first taste of popularity and I'm pretty sure he loved it. Being sighted with Goober immediately became the ultimate sign of coolness. He sat on laps during picnics, flew around the giant tent during the Sean Forrest concert, and joined in the Happy Dance (please tell me you know what the Happy Dance is). You should have seen Goober perched on the shoulders of a 6'2" teenage guy as he danced in praise to Jesus. I bet God loved it.

The only rule was that Goober had to be back in my possession by midnight. That first night, as Goober and I settled into a Little Mermaid sleeping bag (no, it's not mine), the girl next to me began to giggle. "Mrs. C," she laughed, "I've never seen a grownup sleep with a stuffed animal before."

"Welcome to my world, Alex," I smiled. What I didn't say was that Goober helps me feel safe. Have you ever watched as a small child is comforted by his tattered blanket? As long as he's clinging to that blanket, the child rests in confidence that his world is safe. When the child awakens during the night, he reaches through the darkness for the one thing that will soothe him – his blanket.

The child eventually learns that it's God who really keeps him safe, but clinging to that blanket remains a tangible reminder of God's protection. And in his dorky little way, Goober, too, reminds me to cling to God for His protection and love.

Does it make sense? Perhaps not, but it's true. As for a grown woman sleeping with a homely stuffed duck, it has been suggested that I never grew up.

Maybe that's not so bad.

"Unless you become like children, you will never enter the kingdom of heaven." Matt. 18:3

113

Just Another Boring Family Dinner

for Ali Zocco

The college kids were home on break. One brought her roommate, who lived too far away to travel home for the week. Our high school kids had classes during the day but the whole group hung out together at night, making a ridiculous amount of noise. I loved it.

On Sunday morning, we went to Mass. We had to separate the oldest and youngest kids, ages 20 and 14, because they got laughing so hard during the homily that everyone else started giggling, too. We made the mandatory stop for donuts on the way home, arriving at the house just as more teenagers pulled into the driveway. My kids' friends often stop by on Sunday mornings to help us eat the donuts. They're so thoughtful.

Before I knew it, the sun was setting. I did a quick head count for dinner and came up with nine people. Perfect.

Well, sort of. Math whiz that I am, I miscounted. Okay, fine – I forgot one of my own kids. The kid wasn't very happy when she came to the table and found no place to sit, not to mention that there was no food on her nonexistent plate. She thinks family dinners are dumb, anyway, so this didn't help my case.

We were about to say grace when 19-year-old Meredith announced that she'd learned a new grace at college, set to music. We groaned and rolled our eyes. This is a kid who thinks Gregorian chant is the coolest music ever, especially if it's in Latin. I could just imagine what this new grace sounded like.

I needn't have worried. Meredith launched into, "Bless us, O Lord, and these Thy gifts . . ." to the lilting tune of the 'Gilligan's Island' theme song. Pretty cool.

We passed the food around. The youngest kid carefully counted slices of garlic bread to be sure she got her fair share. She never does that with broccoli.

Then someone posed a question. "Suppose you were given $5,000 to spend on yourself. What would you do with it?"

Discussion began immediately. Most of us had no trouble thinking up ways to spend the money. "I'd take that trip to Ireland that I've always dreamed of," said a college kid right away.

"I'd buy a really nice iPod – finally!" said the broccoli kid. "And lots and lots and lots of music, and a big spending spree at the mall! Oh, and a hot tub!"

"You can't get all that for $5,000!" the others yelled.

"Yes, I can," she insisted.

My husband said he'd build a soundproof room. I'm not sure if he wants to blast opera without bothering us, or block out the sounds of his family so he can finally get some quiet. Hey, whatever makes him happy.

Two kids remained silent for the longest time. It turns out that they couldn't think of anything. "Um, well,

I'd buy a skirt for school," one finally began. "Oh, and a new toothbrush, and maybe some socks, and a chocolate bar."

"Isn't there anything big you want?" someone prodded in amazement.

"Well, I might buy a few CD's," she added.

It was the same with the other kid. All she came up with was a pair of jeans, a baseball cap, and some bottled water for her dorm room. When pressed, she said she might splurge on an ice cream sundae.

Someone brought out chocolate chip cookies while others bickered about whose turn it was to do the dishes. In the midst of the commotion, the visiting roommate remarked to no one in particular, "I wish my family had dinner together like this."

Death: The Final Frontier. Or Not.

"I'm not afraid of being dead. I'm just afraid of getting dead."
Marietta Tierney Waite 1959-1993

On April 26, 2006, a Taylor University van with a driver and eight passengers was hit by a huge semi that came barreling across the highway median. Five people in the van were killed. The others were seriously injured.

An EMS veteran and deputy coroner later described the accident as one of the worst scenes he had witnessed in 30 years. The living and the dead were strewn together across the highway along with papers, wallets and debris. In the confusion, the identities of two similar-looking students were switched. It would be five weeks before the terrible error was detected. One of the students in question was alive but in a coma. The other was dead.

Four days after the accident, more than 1,400 people attended the closed-casket funeral for the victim they believed to be Whitney Cerak. Whitney's parents buried her in their hometown of Gaylord, Michigan. Then, they tried to pick up the pieces of their lives.

Back in Fort Wayne, Indiana, the family of Laura VanRyn began a watch by the bedside of a patient they were told was their critically injured daughter. Doctors had warned that they might not recognize her because of the extent of her injuries. For an incredible five weeks, they kept a vigil around the clock.

Serious doubts did not surface until "Laura" began to slowly regain consciousness. In the course of rehabilitation, a therapist asked the patient to write her name. She wrote, "Whitney Cerak." Two days later, her true identity was confirmed with dental records.

This stunning news brought explosive joy to one family, while plunging the other into unparalleled grief. In the ensuing days, the VanRyns had to unearth their daughter's body from a stranger's grave, then rebury her along with their hopes for a future.

How does one heal from such a tragedy? It's like discovering that the child you've been raising was switched in the hospital nursery and actually belongs to someone else, and that your child is dead. Sure, we know that life is unpredictable, but we don't expect life and death to be overturned. After all, alive is alive. Dead is dead.

Or is it?

In truth, isn't death just another phase of life? Doesn't death mark the transition from life on Earth to life with God in heaven? From God's perspective, isn't death less of a separation than it is a doorway?

I'm not suggesting that the death of a loved one is easy. It's not. It's excruciating. God gave us enormous capacity to love, and therefore the death of a loved one leaves a hollow in our hearts that no one else can fill.

God knows this because He, too, suffered the loss of a loved one. It must have been torturous for God to watch His son, even knowing that Jesus would rise again.

The only way we can survive such pain is with hope. As Christians, we have hope of the Resurrection, hope that we will be reunited with our loved ones for all eternity. It is this hope that sustains us after a loved one has died. Without it, we fall into despair.

When Whitney Cerak's parents heard that the girls' identities had been switched and that their daughter was alive, they refused to believe the news. They were terrified that their lives would be shattered yet again. They were afraid to hope.

Are we afraid to hope? Are we afraid that God won't be there to catch us, won't do what He promised, cannot be trusted? In Scripture, we are urged to "hold unswervingly to the hope we profess, for He who promised is faithful." (Heb. 10:23) God is faithful. God deserves our complete trust because God is always faithful.

It's gut-wrenching to watch a loved one suffer and die. It's frightening to face the dying process ourselves. But we always have hope. And that hope will not disappoint us.

Showing Up

for Nancy Setapen Wilber

It was Saturday afternoon and I felt lousy. It wasn't a physical thing; it was more like a deep ache that had been lingering all week, invading my thoughts and disturbing my dreams. Maybe it was more of a longing, or a sadness that I couldn't quite reach.

We had just returned from our annual week on Cape Cod – a noisy week of belly laughs and lazy afternoons floating in mid-tide as the flats stretch out to where they fad into the horizon. There were family tennis competitions and late evening board games and, of course, emergency trips for ice cream.

Just as our vacation began, however, a stomach bug kept me home from Sunday Mass. The rest of the family headed out without me, returning with donuts that I couldn't eat. Fortunately I recuperated in time to enjoy the rest of vacation, but by the following weekend when we returned to Connecticut, nearly two weeks had elapsed since I'd received the Eucharist. I was starving for it, longing for it, aching for it.

You probably think I'm going to tell you that it was glorious when I finally made it to Mass that Sunday.

Unfortunately, it wasn't glorious at all.

My skirt was uncomfortable. My bug bites itched. I was distracted, looking all around as my mind bounced off the walls and ceilings and floor – anywhere except the altar where Jesus was making Himself present to me. So much for a glorious reunion.

A few days later I attended weekday Mass, and again I was distracted and sleepy and inattentive. The Sunday after that, I paid more attention to the new altar servers who wandered around cluelessly, than I paid to the homily and prayers.

What was wrong? Why didn't I feel close to God the way I had in the past? Whatever the problem was, I was sure it was my fault. It's not as if God had moved.

I'm still not sure if I did anything wrong but I know one thing I did right: I did not give up. I kept going to Mass on Sundays with my family, and I kept dragging myself to weekday Mass whenever possible. I also continued my practice of spending one evening a week in prayer in front of the Blessed Sacrament. Even if I couldn't pay attention, I could still show up. Some days that was all I had to offer to God.

It was a hard time. It seemed like God was a million miles away and I had no idea how to reach Him. Fortunately, He knew how to reach me. It happened on a random Tuesday when I filled in as a substitute lector at Mass. The readings were about the Eucharist (why does that not surprise me?). There was nothing different in how I prepared myself that day and yet the words jumped off the page. The homily seemed to be written just for me, with personal touches that no one but God could have known. I couldn't take my eyes off the altar during the consecration, couldn't tear my heart away from prayer after Communion. It was electric. I didn't want to leave.

And so I knelt there, so close to the tabernacle that I could almost touch it, as my heart overflowed with joy. I know God had been with me all along, but there are times when knowledge alone isn't enough. Sometimes we need to feel His touch.

Maybe it's like being in love – sometimes you feel it intensely with fireworks and heart palpitations, and other times there's a benign dullness to the daily routine.

I guess that's how it is with God. We cling to the sure knowledge of God's love, even when He seems far away. We also enjoy those special times when we feel enveloped by His tender embrace. Theoretically, our faith doesn't depend on feelings, but the truth is that we're made of flesh and blood so it's not enough to just grit our teeth and go to Mass. I'm sure God understands.

And so I plod along, sometimes feeling God's tender warmth and sometimes not feeling anything at all. But I continue to show up, even when it's the only thing I have to offer.

How to Annoy a Parish Priest

for church secretaries everywhere

1. Call the rectory late at night to inquire about Mass times. Act surprised when a sleepy person answers the phone.
2. Leave right after Communion. After all, it's important to get a good seat at the local breakfast place.
3. Occasionally forget to show up when you're scheduled to be a lector, usher, or musician. Then complain that he doesn't entrust lay people with enough responsibility.
4. Bug him about restoring one of those 'quick Masses' like they used to have. Tell him that Mass should be in-and-out, just like the car wash.
5. Complain when he preaches about marriage or family. What does he know about that stuff, anyway?
6. Have your mother call the rectory to reserve the church for your wedding. She should make it clear that the date cannot be moved since the reception hall and band have already been booked.
7. Don't volunteer for parish activities. Then complain about how things are done, especially if it was never

done that way before.

8. Buttonhole him just before Mass to describe a lengthy personal problem.

9. Never inquire about his family, hobbies, or vacation plans. It's not as if he's a real person or anything.

10. Wait until the wedding day to invite him to the reception. If he cannot attend, act hurt. If he comes, seat him with the harmless aunts who will bore him mercilessly. Be sure to keep him away from your college buddies; he would never understand youthful indiscretion.

11. Ask him why he gets a day off. He only works one day a week so why does he need a day off?

12. Stick gum under the pews.

13. Threaten to go to a different church if he keeps referring to archaic teachings like chastity and Natural Family Planning. If he hears enough complaints, maybe he'll get with the times.

14. Tell him frequently that you liked the last priest much better.

15. Apologize when you use colorful language in his presence. He probably doesn't realize that you use such words when he's not around.

16. Schedule important parish functions on his day off.

17. Vote against the proposal to air-condition the church and rectory. He wanted to be a priest, and certain inconveniences go with the territory.

18. Show up unannounced at the rectory and demand to see a priest. Why should you need an appointment? They have plenty of time on their hands during the week.

19. Insinuate that he probably doesn't like women since he was willing to forgo marriage in order to be a priest.
20. Nag him about your favorite devotion. Give him all the latest literature and leave flyers around the church.
21. Ask him if you can buy a Mass.
22. When you see him in confession, tell him that you really can't think of any sins to confess since you live alone, and besides, it's not like you killed anybody this week. Explain that you're just there for the graces of the sacrament.
23. When you receive Communion, pluck the host from his hands and walk away.
24. Jiggle your car keys during the homily and the last few minutes of Mass. It's a beautiful sound.
25. Plan a big production wedding that spotlights the bride instead of God.
26. Wait until the last minute to request a sponsor certificate for baptism or confirmation. Be sure to complain if it's not provided immediately.
27. Expect him to be in three places at once.
28. Ask to rent his beautiful church for your wedding. Tell him that you don't need all that religious stuff, especially since you're already living together. You just want a church wedding for the beautiful photos.
29. Register your child for CCD, then act surprised when she's actually expected to attend.
30. Never thank him for making a difference in your life.

No Complaining For How long ???

for Hank Petrilli

It was the summer of 2006 in Kansas City, Missouri, and the Rev. Will Bowen was preparing to deliver a Sunday sermon that would turn his congregation on end.

When Sunday rolled around, Pastor Bowen climbed into the pulpit and began to describe the downward spiral caused by negative speech. He estimated that the average person complains 20 times a day. Multiply that across an entire workforce or family, and the effects are staggering.

Rev. Bowen admitted that he, too, was guilty of complaining. "You name it, I complained about it . . . weather, health, church, friends," he said.

So he issued a challenge: swear off all negative speech for 21 days. No complaining, no criticizing, no gossip, no sarcasm. None.

Pastor Bowen assured them that he was taking the challenge as well.

The minister instructed the ushers to hand out brightly colored rubber bracelets, similar to Lance Armstrong's yellow 'Livestrong' bracelets that were popular a few years ago. He explained that parishioners should place the bracelet on the wrist; each time they complained or criticized, they should switch the bracelet to the opposite wrist and begin counting again. The goal was to make 21 consecutive days with the bracelet in place.

"Join me," he told his congregation. "If it takes three months or three years, your life will be greatly improved. Your relationships will be greatly improved. If you wear your bracelet out, we'll give you another one. Stay with it."

Before the pastor had finished his sermon, he had to switch his own bracelet after complaining about the Kansas City Royals.

Word of the challenge spread quickly. A few weeks later, a reporter asked Rev. Bowen how he was faring. "Me? Well, after two weeks of really trying, I've almost made six hours," he replied honestly.

Slowly, however, he began to make progress, and it led to an interesting observation. "I found that I could do very well around some people but not so well around others. Sadly, I realized that my relationships with some people were centered on expressing our dissatisfaction about whatever we were talking about. I began to avoid them; I felt guilty at first, but I noticed that my bracelet stayed put. More important, I found myself beginning to feel happier."

Rev. Bowen says that the average person who really gives it his best completes the challenge in about five months.

One woman who completed the challenge remarked, "My life is a whole lot better than it was six months ago." This woman was a teacher, and she invited her grade school pupils to take the no-complaints pledge with her.

"It was really hard for me," said a boy in her

classroom, "because I've got two sisters, one 12 and one 13, and they are both," he paused and sighed, "really mean!"

As for me, it's been six weeks since I began the challenge to eliminate negative talk. So far, I've made it nearly two days. To my surprise, I am most likely to fail when I'm driving. This is true even when I'm alone in the car because I criticize other drivers. And yes, this counts as negative speech. The fact that no one can hear me does not change the fact that it has a negative effect on me.

So here is the challenge: go 21 consecutive days without complaints, criticism, sarcasm and gossip. If you have a rubber bracelet, use it. If not, use a wristwatch, rubber band or piece of jewelry. Do it with a friend, or as an office project, or as a family.

Then watch God transform not only your lips, but your heart as well.

"Let no evil talk come out of your mouths, but only such as is good for edifying . . . that it may impart grace to those who hear."
Eph. 4:29

We Love You, Sister Curly

for Mrs. A., Mr. Sallak, Mrs. Delano, and Mr. Harrington, who believed in Meredith before she believed in herself.

Meredith is the second of our four children, and she came tearing into this world entirely bald. I don't mean that she had cute downy fuzz on her scalp. She didn't have so much as a sprig, and what's more, she was very fat. She also had the misfortune of sprouting a mouthful of teeth at an exceptionally early age. The poor kid looked like a piano.

Fortunately she had one huge advantage: Meredith was gorgeous. She's still gorgeous. Even as a baby she would bat her eyelashes at any man with a pulse, flash a fetching grin, and perhaps add a charming gurgle for effect.

It always worked. Meredith never met a man she didn't like, and she had a special penchant for grandfather types. Many spontaneously called her 'Curly,' in honor of the balding member of the Three Stooges. The nickname stuck.

By kindergarten the boys were lining up at the coat hooks to be Meredith's boyfriend. It was not uncommon for a new boy to assume the role just minutes after the predecessor's heart had been broken. The drama continued until more mature romances began in junior high – you know, the kind that takes half the class to orchestrate and lasts about three days.

Meredith is now 20 years old and I'm pleased to report that she sports a beautiful head of hair. The baby fat is a thing of the distant past and she is, in popular lingo, drop-dead gorgeous.

In other words, she's stunning. Oh, and did I mention that she was a Top Ten Scholar in high school? A trained lifeguard, decorated swimmer, Latin and physics scholar, and accomplished artist? And in her spare time, I'm pretty sure she attended every prom ever invented.

So what does a girl like this do with her life?

She enters the convent.

If you think the convent is only for women who can't snag a husband or find a better paying job, think again. The sisters I've met are neither homely nor dull. One of the sisters in Meredith's convent is so spunky that I can picture her as a freckled kid in pigtails, hanging upside down from a climbing tree and pitching acorns at passing schoolmates. Another sister I know could be a brilliant surgeon. As a matter of fact, she is a brilliant surgeon. We're talking about funny, capable, fascinating women.

While many people have greeted Meredith's news with great joy, a surprising number have reacted with disapproval. "You're throwing away your life! You could do so much more!" one person chided, as if there's a calling out there that's more satisfying than saving souls.

Another critic lamented, "I can't believe Meredith is entering the convent. She could have her pick of guys!"

"She does have her pick of guys," I replied with a grin, "and she picked Jesus. Jesus picked her, too. That's what I call a match made in heaven."

The reaction that most irritates me, however, is, "Such a shame. A pretty girl like Meredith . . ." What's the message here – that God only takes ugly women for the convent?

Nothing could be further from the truth.

Consecrated life is not a cosmic booby prize. God creates each person for a particular purpose – single life, marriage, priesthood, religious life – and He writes that purpose into our being from the very beginning.

In Meredith's case, it seems that entering the convent is not so much something she is choosing for herself; it's something for which God created and chose her from the beginning of time.

And so it is that Meredith begins her life at the Capuchin Sisters of Nazareth. May God bless and keep you, my little one. We love you, Sister Curly.

The Question Jar

or

Do Bad Guys Wear Socks?

for Fr. Jeffrey Romans, who touches more lives
than he'll ever know

It started on a cranky afternoon as bickering exploded in my kitchen. A houseful of curious offspring had been asking questions from the moment their tiny feet hit the floor at dawn until they collapsed into bed with their ragged teddy bears at night. One kid was so persistent in her questions that one day I kept count. Even factoring in momentary lapses of quiet, the child asked 392 questions. In a single day.

Most questions were routine and childlike. From time to time, however, a kid asked something that required a thoughtful reply.

Such was the case this particular day. I've long since forgotten the specifics, but I do recall that it deserved more attention than I could give at that moment. So I did what any loving, sensitive parent would do: I hollered at the poor kid. "Write it down and put it into a jar!" I barked. "We'll talk about it later." Thus was born the Question Jar.

Early questions reflected the youth of our children

and the fact that we were in the process of becoming Catholic. "Why does the priest wear white instead of black at a bad guy's funeral?" inquired our 12-year-old. "Why does God love bad guys?" a younger child pondered. "If Santa Claus visits all children everywhere, why are there children in the word who have no toys?" "Why do priests have to go to confession?" "Do bad guys wear socks?"

From time to time at the dinner table, we took out the jar for discussion. The funniest question was, "How are people made?" What our six-year-old wanted to know was, where do babies come from? Peter and I were quite willing to respond, since it was one question to which we actually knew the answer. To our amusement, however, the child insisted that it be answered by family friend, Fr. John Gwozdz. One evening at the dinner table, unsuspecting Father John unfolded the question and read it aloud.

After turning a lovely shade of purple, he swiftly handed the question to us.

Another time that same child asked, "Why do we have belly buttons?" The older kids started to giggle but before we could respond, she blurted out her own explanation. "Oh, I know! It's so we can do the back float!"

We erupted in laughter, but she paid no mind. "My swimming teacher says that to do the back float, I have to put my belly button into the air," she explained with childish innocence. "That's why we have belly buttons – so we can do the back float!"

As the years progressed, questions grew more sophisticated. "Can angels sin?" "Did the Virgin Mary experience pain during labor?" And one question that kept us going for months: "Are people basically good or basically evil? If they are good, why do we sin? If they are evil, how can God have made us in His image?" And then there was my personal favorite, "Why are Polish men so obstinate, and why do so many become priests?"

From time to time, a group of priest friends gathers here for dinner, and invariably someone pulls out the Question Jar. Fr. Jeffrey Romans always peruses the contents of the jar when he thinks no one is looking. He snatches a few questions for himself, hands the clinkers to his brother priests, and stuffs back into the jar those he doesn't want to discuss that evening. Some questions are neglected for a year or more, but ultimately every query receives attention, even if we have to pull out Bibles, the Catechism, and laptop to ensure accuracy.

The kids are now older teens and young adults, and again, the sophistication of the questions reflects their maturity. In recent years, questions have included such topics as Natural Family Planning, the role of women in the Church, and what happens to devout Muslims after death. The last time I pulled out the Question Jar, two kids groaned, "Not that thing again!" And yet within minutes, they were immersed in a heated debate about whether the Book of Revelation can be taken literally. This was followed by a discussion of whether Harry Potter books promote witchcraft or should be enjoyed as good fiction.

I love our Question Jar. Nowadays, many of the questions are written by me. The jar serves as a reminder that I have much to learn about the faith, and it encourages me to seek God with all of my mind. Knowledge isn't everything, but it's an important start.

What Do You Have in Your Hand?

for Joe Martin, with a kiss

I was nearly out of my mind. I was in a meeting for an important project, but one person on the committee was driving everyone crazy. This lady jiggled her leg, tapped her foot, paced around the room, and when called on, seemed distracted and scattered. She acted as if she had Attention Deficit Disorder, a difficulty in focusing and organizing one's thoughts, usually associated with school-age children. I knew she had even tried medication to treat the problem but nothing had helped. Instead, she just drove everyone crazy.

The most frustrating thing was that I could never get away from this lady. Why? The woman is me.

I wasn't always this way. My childhood was filled with orderliness and books – lots and lots of books. Back then, my concentration was fine, and if anything needed organizing, I was the one to call.

But years earlier, a medical emergency robbed my brain of oxygen, leaving me with impaired ability to read, follow sequences and organize.

It's incredibly frustrating. "I could do so much

more!" I complain to God as often as possible. "If only I could keep track of things, if only I could read. Just think how much I could accomplish! Instead, I am so limited."

And God asks in reply, "What do you have in your hand?"

Huh?

Then I remember. Back in the Old Testament, the Israelites were an unruly bunch. When God appeared to Moses in the burning bush to tell him to lead the Jews out of bondage, Moses was skeptical. Moses saw only the obstacles – and there were many. God, however, was not concerned with obstacles. He didn't want to know what Moses couldn't do; He wanted to know what Moses was willing to do.

"What do you have in your hand?" God asked Moses at a particularly stubborn juncture in the conversation. Moses' reply was something along the lines of, "Just this big, ugly stick." So God zapped the stick and turned it into a serpent, which Moses used to convince the Israelites to follow him out of Egypt.

So again God asks me, "What do you have in your hand?"

God is not concerned with what I don't have or cannot do. He wants to know what I can do, and what I'm willing to do. What can I offer to Him?

Fast forward several years. I was at the grocery store, contemplating the chocolate Teddy Grahams in aisle three, when an acquaintance stopped to say hello. This woman looked stunning as always, with perfect clothes, perfect makeup, perfect hair. She was married to a prominent surgeon with a Colgate smile, and together they had two beautiful children and an exquisite home. On weekends, they did volunteer work with the underprivileged.

It all looked pretty perfect to me.

So I was surprised when, after a few pleasantries, she blurted out, "You have such a perfect family."

What? Did I hear her correctly? She knew only what she saw at Mass on Sunday mornings when we were well-scrubbed and well-behaved. Even then, my younger children bickered in the sacristy about whose turn it was to light the candles, while the older kids slouched and sulked in the pew. All she saw was the veneer, the exterior of our lives, and she concluded that the family is perfect. It's not.

"I am very blessed," I said honestly, "but believe me, we have our share of problems."

"No, you don't," she stated emphatically, as if her future rested on believing her own words. "Your family is perfect. Your life is perfect."

I was shocked. What did she know about my life? I didn't feel that I owed her an account of my problems, but neither did I want to be dismissed as some stained-glass saint who waltzes effortlessly through life on gilded wings.

"My life isn't perfect at all," I insisted. "I battle arthritis, thyroid disease and mental illness. I have trouble reading. We deal with teenage and family issues. Sometimes life is really hard."

Yeah, right, perfect life, I thought to myself. If life were really perfect, I'd be able to curl up with a good book. I wouldn't walk with a cane. If my life were perfect I could accomplish so much more . . .

And again I remembered. "What do you have in your hand?"

137

Not much, Lord. And I have a beat-up body and a leaky mind.

I'm not positive, but I'm pretty sure that God replied, "Sounds good to Me. Now let's see how we can put those to good use."

Wisdom from the First Fifty Years

for Deacon Martin Jacques, my hero

I recently reached the milestone birthday of half a century, which prompted me to muse about what I have learned over the years . . .

1. Never go from one room to another empty-handed.
2. Teach your young son to be a gentleman, even if you have to use bubble gum to bribe him. By the time he's 20, he'll be the most popular guy on campus.
3. If you have to give someone constructive criticism, do it orally, NOT in writing. Keep it brief.
4. When you have positive feedback to deliver, do it in writing. You may want to give a copy to the person's supervisor as well.
5. Never lie. Never. There is no such thing as a white lie. If it would break a confidence to answer someone's question, simply decline to answer. But never lie. Never.
6. Do not treat the oldest child with unreasonable

strictness, nor allow the youngest child to be undisciplined. And be sure to take photos of younger children.

7. Sign up for every possible carpool during your kids' teen years. If you're quiet enough as you drive, they'll forget you're there.

8. Count how many times you complain or criticize in one week. If it's more than three, it's too often.

9. Attend wakes and funerals. You will never regret paying respects to a loved one or to his family.

10. Memorize your parents' birthdays. You'll be surprised how many times the information comes in handy.

11. Don't let your kids date until they are 16, and make yours the home where teens hang out. It will cost you in groceries, but it's cheaper than drug treatment or family therapy.

12. Pray. God loves to hear your voice.

13. If you can't think of anything nice to say, don't say anything. Even if what you're saying is true, it's still gossip if it's unkind.

14. Never interrupt a compliment.

15. Visit your grandmother in the nursing home. If you no longer have a grandmother, visit someone else's grandmother.

16. Treat everyone with kindness, including people you don't like. Especially people you do not like.

17. Breastfeed.

18. If you're married, go on a date once a week. It doesn't have to be anything fancy; just a weekly time together.

19. Tithe. It's easier to live on 90% of your income than it is to live on 100%.
20. Never complain to someone's supervisor until you have first directed your concern to the person himself or herself. And keep it civil. ALWAYS keep it civil.
21. Let your kids take risks. Then let them bear the consequences.
22. Go to confession at least once a month. More if you're married.
23. Don't give an instruction to a child unless you plan to enforce it. And when you do give an instruction, don't ask the child if it's okay. It's usually not okay with the child, but that's life.
24. Donuts help make everything a little bit better.
25. Use sunscreen. If you die from a lightening strike, so be it, but dying because you can't be bothered to use sunscreen is shameful.
26. "Use it up, wear it out, make it do, or do without." My grandmother was one smart lady.
27. Use cloth diapers, and launder them yourself. Yes, I'm serious.
28. St. Jerome said, "Ignorance of the Bible is ignorance of Christ." No kidding.
29. Don't sleep with your boyfriend or girlfriend before marriage. Make up for lost time after you're married.
30. Exercise.
31. If your parents are still alive, call or visit each week.
32. Teach your kids that life is not fair. Sometimes

there are four kids and only three lollipops. The sooner they learn this, the better.

33. Go to Mass every Sunday, and get there 10 minutes early to settle yourself in. Stay for a few minutes after it's over.

34. Recycle.

35. Married couples, use Natural Family Planning. It's not messy, intrusive, or risky. It binds together husband and wife, is extremely effective, and it drastically reduces the likelihood of divorce. What's not to like?

36. If your destination is less than a mile, walk.

37. Treat teenagers like real human beings – because they are real human beings.

38. At the end of a long, successful career, no one ever laments, "I wish I had spent more time in meetings." Too often, however, people regret, "I wish I had spent more time with my family."

39. Never be ashamed of the Gospel.

Getting in Touch with my Inner June Cleaver

for Tenna

Family vacation – *n.*, 1. a quaint but archaic notion that one can relax in the presence of tiny children. 2. The opportunity to cook on someone else's stove.

I should have known that this vacation was going to be trouble. To start with, we couldn't find the place. It took an hour of wandering up and down the rutted dirt road before we stumbled upon a dilapidated shack in the woods. My friend had described the place as 'quaint'; she hadn't mentioned that the architectural design resembled an outhouse.

When we stepped inside, my fears were confirmed. It was not quaint; it was miniscule. Picture a pup tent with plumbing.

Oh, and did I mention that there were 23 of us staying there?

This was my introduction to Cape Cod vacations. Still, we were young and foolish and without children so I must admit, the weekend was great fun, if a tad crowded.

The problem was that Peter fell in love with the place. It sat atop a dune overlooking the Brewster flats in Cape Cod, Massachusetts. At high tide, the beach below was large enough to take a snooze or play Frisbee. At low tide, you could walk out for nearly a mile among the hermit crabs and minnows and clam shells. The locale was spectacular.

My concern was that someday we hoped to have children, and this place was hardly family-friendly. I could just imagine a kid slipping out the rotted screen door in the dead of night, toddling toward open ocean. Alone. In diapers.

The cabin itself was three rooms with no amenities whatsoever; no tub or shower, no wall boards or curtains or rugs to dampen sound, no appliances except a tiny stove and an occasionally working 1940s Frigidaire. There was no TV, no radio, no telephone. Ancient wiring was exposed, creating an enticing playground for teething babies. The mattresses of two lumpy beds sloped steeply toward huge craters in the center.

The owner of the cottage was a tough old Yank who was so paranoid about intruders that she'd planted poison ivy up and down the dirt road and surrounding the cabin. As a consequence, the place was not only nearly impossible to find, but if you did find it, you couldn't get near it. If you were inside, you couldn't escape.

And no, I'm not making any of this up.

Eventually we established the tradition of vacationing on Cape Cod for a week each summer, and sure enough, we settled upon the spacious accommodations of Outhouse Cottage. One summer when we had three preschoolers, it rained for six of the seven days. The following year, Hurricane Bob was our companion for the week, which meant we had neither running water nor electricity. Then there were the years when Peter was in training for triathlons. He enjoyed 50-mile training rides and long ocean swims while I romped in the poison ivy with four small children. It would have been funny if it weren't so awful.

I finally pleaded with Peter for a change of venue. All I wanted were a few basic amenities – you know, things like wall boards. (And people think women are so high-maintenance.) I was quite willing to return to the rustic charm of the poison ivy once everyone was out of diapers, but hey, even June Cleaver needed a rest sometime.

Thus, we found ourselves in a more civilized environment, with an indoor shower and working refrigerator. The irony is that Peter became so enamored of the creature comforts that we never returned to Outhouse Cottage.

As our children grew, our annual summer vacation gradually became more bearable. In fact, nowadays it's a high point of the year. Honestly, I never thought it would happen.

Last summer marked a new era. It was our first night on Cape Cod, and we gathered for dinner amidst noisy laughter and dish towel fights and the singing of grace. Then our daughter-in-law cleared her throat and we fell oddly silent. To our delight, she and our son announced that they were expecting a baby. Cheers erupted. Our youngest kid dubbed the baby, 'Lil Pablo.'

The following March, we welcomed our first

grandbaby, Maranatha Grace Cram. Six weeks later, the college kids drove 19 hours round-trip so they could be here for the baptism. The baby spent the day in the arms of adoring relatives and friends, who formed a waiting line to hold her.

As I watched, it occurred to me that Peter and I did it all wrong during those years when the children were small. We should have vacationed with aunts and grandparents. Then I could have relaxed on the beach sipping iced tea, while family members chased toddlers and basked in the rustic charm of the waterfront poison ivy.

The Last Cell Phone Holdout

for Tina Ryba

"If nominated, I will not accept; if elected, I will not serve." Gen.
William Tecumseh Sherman

"I'll call you when these are ready," the clerk tells
me, tying the shirts together. "What's your cell phone
number?" "I don't have one," I reply.

The clerk stares at me in disbelief. "How can you live
without a cell phone?"

"I like it this way," I reply. "I don't want an electronic
leash."

"But what if I need to reach you?" the woman
presses.

"We're talking about dry cleaning," I say, my
patience ebbing. "What kind of emergency are you
expecting?"

Cell phones. They used to be a luxury for the rich.
Now they're considered essential for anyone with a pulse.

I have no moral objection to cell phones. I simply do
not view them as urgently required for intelligent life on
the planet. Evidently I define 'necessity' differently from
most.

I work at home. My college kids live on a small campus. My high school kids are nearby and have predictable schedules. Would a cell phone occasionally make life easier? Sure. But do I place it in the same category as food, shelter, and coffee? I do not. As a consequence, we have not provided cell phones for our adorable offspring.

By the cries of pain in the Cram household, you'd think that I refused to give my children Easter candy.

Perhaps the most frustrating aspect of this issue is that nearly all adults side with the children, especially after the kids begin to drive. "You'll change your mind when your daughter gets her license," friends warn. "I mean, what if she has an accident? What if she gets lost?"

My answer is annoyingly simply. Automobiles became commonplace in the 1920s. Cell phones became popular in the 1990s. This means that people drove cars for 70 years in luxurious quiet. As far as I know, the system worked reasonably well most of the time.

Our solution is to tell the kids that if anyone wants a cell phone, by all means, get one. And pay for it yourself.

Can you hear the grumbles?

Personally I hope to go to my grave without a cell phone. I dislike the telephone. I don't want to be found easily, and sometimes the only peace and quiet I get is in the car as I retrieve kids from sports practices. Why would I want to shatter that silence with a device that I don't like?

Recently I had a bad day that reinforced my distaste for the telephone. It began with several phone calls from a youth group kid needing advice. Then a friend called, frustrated that her teen's English teacher assigned sexually explicit books to read – at a Catholic school.

A doctor called. A kid's coworker phoned to swap shifts. My son called for information on Holy Day Masses. One wrong number. One call from hubby to ask about my life of leisure.

Have I mentioned that I hate the telephone?

After dinner, I slipped out of the house and headed to the church, where I reveled in front of the Blessed Sacrament. I love the dark and the quiet and the pleasure of Jesus' company. I stayed for hours.

I arrived home late, after everyone was asleep. A note on the whiteboard alerted me to a package on the kitchen counter. The small box was labeled with my name and emblazoned with the brand, 'Sprint.' It was a gift from my family – my very own cell phone.

I said some bad words.

Have I mentioned that I hate the telephone?

I've had the phone for two months and have used it a total of six and a half minutes, none of which were particularly voluntary. I keep it in the glove compartment of the car, where it's not likely to bother me. I've resisted learning the phone number since I don't want anyone to call me. I certainly won't be one of those people whose cell phone interrupts a concert or wedding. Don't get me started about the guy who actually took a call during a funeral, chatting away until the priest stared him down.

Feel free to write a letter to me with stories of how much you love your cell phone. Tell me how your cell phone saved a drowning guppy or rescued your child from a detention. I will read your letter in luxurious quiet, which suits me just fine.

Whatever the Cost

for Marie Shoup

Two weeks ago I drove to the small town of Tunkhannock, Pennsylvania to hand over my eldest daughter to a small convent of Capuchin sisters. Meredith is spending a month there as a candidate, and if all goes as planned, she will formally enter the convent as a postulant in the fall. It's all very exciting.

To be honest, however, it's bittersweet. Our close-knit family is watching as our beloved Meredith makes a new life without us. Everyone is feeling the sacrifice.

Several times recently in front of the Blessed Sacrament, I've considered this sacrifice, this cost of discipleship. Last week with only Jesus as my companion in the darkened church, I totally melted down. "I've given up so much, Lord!" I sobbed to my heavenly Father. "I battle mental illness, thyroid disease, arthritis. My memory doesn't work, I can't read, can't pay attention, and now I'm supposed to give up my child? How much do you want?!!"

And in that quiet place I'm quite sure I heard His reply: "Everything. I want everything."

That's when it occurred to me that God gave up His Child, too. It's not as if He doesn't understand total, unconditional sacrifice. In a very real way, God asks such sacrifice of each of us. "Will you, or will you not follow Me, even when it takes you to places you'd rather not go?" He asks in love. "Who is in charge of your life, anyway?" Put another way, who controls the channel flipper?

Dietrich Bonhoeffer, a minister who died in a Nazi death camp, said it even more starkly. "When Christ calls a man, He bids him come and die." For there is no partial Gospel. We cannot say 'yes' to God in moderation. To follow Christ is to die to self, and one cannot be partially dead any more than one can be partially pregnant. To truly follow Christ is a radical thing, a counter-cultural thing.

It's also a Catholic thing.

On the surface, being a Christian doesn't look so hard. Try to love people, go to church, be a good person, and that's about it.

But that's not it at all. We have lived this bland version of Christianity for so long that we actually think it's the real thing. In truth, it bears little resemblance to the Christianity that Jesus preached and lived. In essence, Jesus said that if we're not upsetting the apple cart, we're probably not living the Gospel. Anyone can go to church. It takes guts to take it with us when we leave.

Let me be blunt. Just going to Mass is not enough. God wants more than our attendance; He wants our hearts. He wants a relationship with us. He wants us to be madly, passionately in love with Him, just as He is with us.

He wants us to act like young lovers preparing for a lifetime together, not like customers buying laundry detergent at Wal-Mart.

God wants total surrender, not just weekend

visitation.

The cost can be steep. It will mean an end to our prejudices – even the ones we consider harmless. We will have to forgo our bigotry toward people of other races, and those who sport tattoos or dreadlocks, and those who are gay. This radical obedience will change the way we look at the very rich and the desperately poor, those who need medical insurance or a living wage or a place to live until they get back on their feet. It will involve a painful return to chastity before marriage, and a commitment to treat our elderly with dignity.

Total surrender to Jesus will mean that our soup kitchens will be empty, our forgiveness will be unconditional, and the lines for confession will be long.

Like the woman caught in adultery and the leper who was healed, encountering Jesus changes us forever. It will be awesome and difficult and sometimes pathetic, but it will never be boring.

Total surrender to God will change us forever – all the way into eternity.

Service of Love

for Al and Adrienne Keogler

It was the most menial job in a household, typically relegated to the lowliest servant. In fact, in some places during the first century A.D., this task was considered so demeaning that a master could not compel a servant to perform it.

What was this degrading task? Washing feet.

It's no surprise, therefore, that the apostles balked when Jesus washed their feet at the Last Supper. Why was the Master on His knees like an ordinary slave? It made them terribly uncomfortable.

Jesus' message to His followers was clear: in order to be His disciple, one must serve. This was non-negotiable. It's still non-negotiable.

* * * * * * * *

I was driving down historic Main Street in my hometown, enjoying the warm sun and the delightful silence. An electronic ring tone pierced my tranquility. It was my cell phone – the one my family gave me despite my noisy objections.

"Hi, Sweetheart," I said cheerfully to Tierney, my pragmatic 21-year-old daughter.

"Mom! Mom! Mom! Mom! Mom! Mom!" Tierney squealed into the phone.

I knew what she was going to tell me.

Tierney and her boyfriend, Andrew, had been enjoying an afternoon date – a rare treat amid the demands of college classes and jobs. Andrew had begun the date by bringing Tierney to an empty church some distance from his family home. There they spent 10 or 15 minutes in silent prayer, and then prayed a rosary together. This was followed by more silent prayer. By the time Andrew launched into the Stations of the Cross, Tierney had grown restless. Why weren't they heading out on their date? I mean, prayer is great, but enough is enough.

After more than an hour in the church, Andrew suggested that they say a final prayer in front of the statue of the Blessed Mother, where a spectacular bouquet of red roses was displayed. "Then can we leave?" Tierney silently grumbled.

They offered a brief prayer, and Tierney turned to depart.

"Wait," Andrew said.

What now?

As Tierney faced him, Andrew dropped to one knee, opened a small velvet box, and quietly asked, "Tierney, will you marry me?"

Tierney gasped, then stared at the box, dumbfounded, before finding her voice. "Yes!" she exclaimed.

The young couple talked quietly for a moment before

Andrew asked Tierney to take a seat in a nearby pew. She watched as he walked to the pulpit, stooped behind it, and pulled out a bowl of water and a towel. Andrew then knelt in front of Tierney, removed her shoes, and proceeded to wash her feet.

Once again, the symbolism was clear. Their marriage would be a life of service, and that service would begin with Andrew.

When I related this story to some married friends, the husband groaned. "Oh, great. Now my wife is going to expect me to serve her!" he said with more seriousness than jest.

"Your wife *should* expect you to serve her," I replied. "And hopefully your wife will serve you as well. Isn't that part of loving, honoring, and cherishing? And isn't marriage a crucible for living out the Gospel?"

Many of us take decades to learn this truth. Tierney and Andrew are doing it right from the start.

Oh, the roses in front of the Blessed Mother were for Tierney.

I Can Walk

for Mary Regina Martin, who kept me going

It happens often. I'll be taking a brisk walk around the block in inclement weather when a neighbor stops to chat. "Why are you walking in this awful weather?" the neighbor invariably asks. 'This awful weather' can mean heat, cold, snow, rain, or any variety of New England storm.

My honest answer is, 'Because I can.'

But that's not what I say. I mumble something about enjoying the exercise, getting fresh air, endorphins . . . that sort of thing. If I'm speaking with a friend, I may explain that a few years ago, I had to start medications that packed 60 pounds on me, and I am determined to work it off.

But that still doesn't explain why I walk. I walk because I can.

I grew up with an active lifestyle. I was always reasonably fit, and my family was active as well. It was all I knew.

This good fortune carried me through most of my life, including four pregnancies. Then, eight years ago, an auto-immune form of arthritis invaded my life.

The arthritis was a real shocker for me. It crept in

slowly at first, mimicking a rotator cuff injury – except that I hadn't injured my rotator cuff. Before long, the other shoulder was in pain. Then, it was thumbs, and a hip, and lower back. Within six months, I was riddled with crippling arthritis. I bought a cane to help me walk. I got a handicapped tag for my car. We started to think about wheelchairs. The pain quickly became unbearable.

At its worst, I could only sleep an hour or two at a time. Pain would force me out of bed in the dark of night, and I'd pace the halls for nearly an hour until the piercing spasms subsided. Then I'd crawl back into bed and the cycle would begin again.

One particular morning, I was curled up on the sofa, exhausted from another fractured night. A priest friend stopped by the house to go running with my husband Peter, and to bring me Communion. As I received that Precious Body, I was moved to tears that Jesus would come to me in the midst of discouragement and pain.

A moment later, the crushing spasms returned. I hauled myself off the couch, hunched over my cane and began my slow, uneven trudge around the house, quietly sobbing. There might have been a thousand people around me, but I could not have felt more alone. I was so demoralized by the pain.

Eventually the doctors prescribed a new, injectable medication for me. Within a week, I was sleeping through the night. A few months later, I placed the cane into the trunk of the car. It gets very little use these days.

Still, it was years before I could walk any distance. Gradually, imperceptibly, however, I was able to press a tad further than the day before. At first it was just a house or two, then a few more. The day finally arrived when I exploded with excitement to Peter. "Guess what? I walked around the whole block, all by myself!"

By 2009, I'd extended my walks to other neighborhoods. I began parking on the far end of parking lots when shopping. I run errands on foot if the distance is less than a mile or two. I revel in every step.

That same year, my niece gave me a pedometer. My husband jokes that I wear the pedometer to bed, and the sad truth is that I actually do. I literally never take it off except to shower. I love it because it provides a seven-day history of my steps. Experts consider a healthy goal to be 10,000 steps per day. My goal these days is 12,000.

I love this renewed ability to walk. It's not just the endorphins and the fresh air; I love that I am physically able to walk. I love the feel of the pavement under my feet and the smell of pine needles along woodland paths. I love the second chance that God has bestowed upon me, not because I deserve it but simply because He loves to bless His children.

So if you ask me why I walk, I may mutter something about an exercise regimen or staying in shape, but that's not really it all.

I walk because I can. And for this, I give all the glory to God.

Radical Forgiveness

for Judy Santostefano

I was hopping mad as I left Mass at my friend's parish. It was the 10th anniversary of Sept. 11, and the Mass readings were all about forgiveness. In fact, Jesus made it plain that God will forgive us only if we forgive others. That's scary stuff.

The priest mentioned the events of 9/11, then preached about the importance of forgiving family and friends who have hurt us.

There was no mention of forgiving the terrorists.

Later in the Mass, we offered prayers for those who died in the 9/11 attacks. We prayed for their families, the first responders, survivors, and all victims of terrorism around the world.

We did not pray for the terrorists.

We didn't pray for them 10 years ago, either. Once again, I ask the question that I distinctly remember asking back then: if we are commanded to love our enemies and pray for those who persecute us, why don't we pray for the bad guys? Why wasn't Osama Bin Laden's name among the prayers for the dead after U. S. forces destroyed his villa? Why don't we pray for the movie theater shooter in

Colorado? Why don't we pray for Al Qaeda terrorists and neo-Nazis and school shooters?

I'll grant you that it is extremely difficult to pray for such evil men. People will jump to the conclusion that we are excusing their actions, which we most certainly are not. But if Jesus commanded us to forgive 70 times 7, to love our enemies and to pray for those who persecute us, just when do we plan to start?

Many people hesitate to forgive because they mistakenly believe that forgiving someone releases that person from responsibility or guilt. In fact, it does nothing of the sort. Neither does the act of forgiving mean that we condone the action. Rather, offering forgiveness releases us from the grip of rage so that neither the offense nor the perpetrator has any more power over us. The whole mess becomes God's problem instead of ours.

Another incorrect belief is that God calls us to forgive and forget. The truth is that nowhere in Scripture do we find this phrase. We cannot make ourselves forget the intense pain from betrayal, divorce, abuse, or abandonment. In human terms, it is impossible to forget such pain. We are commanded, however, to forgive the person who inflicted the pain. In so doing, we are freed from its terrible grasp so we can begin to heal.

Personal pain can be harder to forgive than global pain. We may more readily forgive a terrorist than the person who broke up our marriage. The former is impersonal; the latter is intensely personal, maybe even intentional. It takes supernatural grace to forgive such a person, and yet this is precisely what we are called to do. Forgive the spouse who cheated on you. Forgive the family member who wreaks havoc, and the man who abused you, and the friend who betrayed you.

Forget? Not likely. In fact, you may need to steer clear of the offending person in order to maintain physical and emotional safety. Legal action may be required. Nevertheless, Jesus says to love our enemies and to pray for those who persecute us. This means to forgive, and forgive, and when we think we cannot do it any more, forgive again.

This Christianity stuff is radical; it's no wonder that so many people deserted Jesus. Following Christ is hard, and anyone who says otherwise probably isn't doing it right.

So we forgive others for their offenses. We love our enemies and pray for those who persecute us. These actions may be the hardest things we ever do, but they will produce a peace in our souls that can only be found in Christ.

Time to start.

What I Did on My Summer Vacation

Warning: If you are squeamish about bats or needles, you may want to skip this story.

I had just returned home from a delightful evening of prayer. I greeted the crowd of college students at the house, kissed my kids good-night, and crawled into bed next to my husband.

As I drifted into sleep, shrieks of terror jolted me upright. "A bat! A bat! A bat! A bat!" kids screamed repeatedly. Downstairs, two girls dove under the kitchen table, naively thinking this would protect them from a creature with sonar. A third student was swiping the air with a large bedspread in a vain attempt to trap the bat. Two more were doubled over in uproarious laughter.

"Reg, it's a bat!" several students shouted to me, as if I hadn't heard the commotion. "Mom, catch it!" begged a kid under the table.

"You cannot catch a bat at night," I explained to the wide-eyed youths. "Bats fly too quickly, and since they use echolocation to navigate, they'll always stay out of reach. Just ignore it. We'll find it in the morning when it's asleep, and then we'll call Animal Control to get rid of it."

Eventually, the guests departed and our kids headed to bed. Fortunately, our offspring had the sense to close their bedroom doors. Do you think this occurred to me? Oh, no. To make matters worse, when Peter got up during the night, he was nicked or bitten by the flying critter.

The next morning, intense searching revealed what is surely the ugliest creature ever designed by God. It was sound asleep in the folds of the living room drapes. We called the Animal Control officer, described the location of the bat, and informed household members that the officer would arrive within an hour or two. Then Peter and I headed to work. Neither of us was at home when the officer knocked at our door.

And knocked. And knocked. The door was open but no one answered her loud calls. The problem was that the Animal Control officer is not allowed to enter a residence unless the homeowner personally invites her in. In the absence of a live body, the law requires a police escort.

So, the officer called the local police, who arrived with sirens screeching and light bar ablaze.

Inside the house, police and Animal Control officers conferred in the kitchen. It was at that moment that 16-year-old Victoria arose after sleeping late. Knowing nothing about the bat, she stepped out of her room and looked into the faces of three uniformed officers standing in her kitchen. She nearly shot her hands into the air and shouted, "I didn't do it!" She had slept through the entire episode. That girl can sleep.

Without incident, the offending critter was carted away for rabies testing, and our family departed for our

Cape Cod vacation.

A few days later, Peter received a disturbing telephone call from the Animal Control officer. Evidently, the bat's brain had partially liquified so there was insufficient material to test for rabies.

The implication of this news was serious: we had to assume that the bat was rabid. Peter had been scratched or bitten, and we'd both slept with an open door, placing me at risk as well. Since the survival rate for rabies is zero, it was urgent that we begin treatment right away.

Reluctantly, Peter and I packed up on a steamy August night and headed for Cape Cod's only large hospital. Did I mention that it's the only large hospital, in the height of tourist season? There were plenty of emergencies on Cape Cod that evening, so we were hardly on the staff's priority list.

Hours passed before Peter and I were ushered into lovely his-and-her hospital green emergency department cubbies. More time passed. Finally, a nurse approached, toting a needle the size of a shish kabob skewer. "This will hurt a little," she understated as fire ricocheted through my back side. Four more doses followed.

Aren't summer vacations fun?

In the ensuing weeks, Peter and I received additional shots, which could only be dispensed at local hospitals. For some reason, staff members always found our situation funny.

The real fun began when we had to explain the whole thing to the insurance company. Rabies treatment costs the equivalent of the Gross National Product of a small country – all for an ugly flying mammal.

Scripture assures us that eventually, every knee shall bend and every tongue confess that Jesus Christ is Lord. Do bats have knees and tongues? I hope so. It would make me feel better about the wretched ordeal.

Sleep Tight, Little One

for John Thomas

The little stick turned pink. She was pregnant.

The news was met with joyful fear, or perhaps fearful joy. After all, they were barely scraping by as a family of three; how would they manage another baby? Still, Oliver and Johanna wanted this new child. They were just frightened. Johanna worked full-time. Oliver worked part-time and was also a full-time graduate student. Together they cared for their young toddler with help from grandparents. The couple had very little money but they shared a deep faith in God's saving love.

From the outset of the pregnancy, Johanna was terribly nauseous. Whoever termed it 'morning sickness' was surely not a mother. It was morning-noon-and-night sickness, and this woman had it all. It was especially hard to care for an active toddler while she felt so poorly.

Not far into the pregnancy, an ultrasound yielded startling news: Johanna was carrying twins. Again, the news was met with joy and fear. How could they feed two more mouths while Oliver was still in grad school? How could Johanna leave behind two nursing babies when she returned to work? And yet, they were awed by the wonder of these tiny gifts from God, who surely would provide for them. Family and friends pitched in with meals and child care so the expectant mom could get extra sleep. Everyone prayed a lot.

As this drama unfolded, I had a front row seat. You see, Peter and I are the grandparents, and you can be sure that the news of twin grandbabies was met with tremendous joy. Our three college kids were equally excited, playfully bickering about who would be the favorite auntie. I mean, twins in the family!

My only concern was whether the other grandmother and I would have the energy to care for two babies plus a toddler. After all, there's a reason that 50-year-old women don't have babies. (One wag said it's because we'd put them down and forget where we put them.) Nevertheless, it was a delightful problem. Our friends envied us.

The excitement was short-lived. One sun-filled afternoon when Johanna came by the house to pick up her chatty toddler, her eyes brimmed with tears. "We lost one of the babies," she sobbed. The doctor had offered no explanation; the young life simply stopped.

We were told that it happens a lot. In fact, many doctors believe that the majority of twin pregnancies ultimately yields only one baby.

This knowledge did not soothe the grief. Neither was I comforted by the fact that I, too, had lost a twin during one of my pregnancies, later delivering a healthy singleton. We clung to the hope that Oliver and Johanna's remaining baby would continue without harm.

Gradually, the couple grew accustomed to their

painful loss as they prepared for the baby she carried. As summer dawned, Johanna gave birth to a beautiful, healthy baby boy. His arrival was met with a tremendous outpouring of joy.

But I'd be lying if I said it was joy alone. It was joy laced with sadness as we mourned the child whom we never met. A previous grandbaby had also died during pregnancy, adding to the people I look forward to meeting in heaven.

When friends ask how many grandchildren we have, I answer, "Two." Silently I add, "and two in heaven."

Sleep tight, little one. I'm saving up kisses until we meet in glory.

Made in the USA
Charleston, SC
19 October 2014